The Appin Murder

Angus Matheson
M.A.

A Traditional Account reprinted
from Vol. XXXV of the Transactions
of the Gaelic Society of Inverness

CLUB LEABHAR — INBHIRNIS

The Publishers gratefully acknowledge permission to
publish 'The Appin Murder' granted by The Gaelic
Society of Inverness and Mrs F. C. Matheson, Edinburgh.
Le taing dhuibhse uile.

Dealbh-sgail: Alex Hendry

Air fhoillseachadh le Club Leabhar Ltd, Inbhirnis
Air a' chlo-bhualadh le John G. Eccles, Inbhirnis

A TRADITIONAL ACCOUNT OF THE APPIN MURDER.

During the last Jacobite rising, of 1745-46, Dugald Stewart, 10th of Appin, was a minor, and the Stewart brigade, 360 strong at Prestonpans, was commanded by Charles Stewart, 5th of Ardsheil (Teàrlach Mór Aird Seile), a famous swordsman, traditionally reputed to be the first man to have wounded Rob Roy in single combat. After the rising was suppressed, Ardsheil was attainted, and, after many adventures while lurking in the West Country, he succeeded in escaping to France, where he died at Sens on 15th May, 1757.

After his flight, his estates were managed in the interest of his widow and children by his bastard half-brother, James Stewart (born c. 1695[1]), who established himself on the farm of Glenduror, and was known as James of the Glen (Seumas a' Ghlinne). James had been an officer in the Stewart brigade during the rising but, as the part he had played was a minor

3

one, he was pardoned under the Act of Indemnity. He was evidently a man of considerable ability and natural gifts for leadership, and, in the absence of his brother Ardsheil, he tacitly assumed headship in the district.

In 1748 Colin Campbell of Glenure was recommended as factor, and on February 23, 1749, he was appointed factor on the estates of Ardsheil, Callart, and that part of the estate of Lochiel holding of the Duke of Gordon (Mamore). That the factor should be a strong Hanoverian was to be expected, but the choice of a Campbell for Stewart territory was not happy.

Colin Campbell was the eldest son of Patrick Campbell of Barcaldine and Glenure by his second wife, Lucy, daughter of the famous Sir Ewen Cameron of Lochiel. He had been a Lieutenant in Loudon's Regiment and had served against the Jacobites, but was not present at the battle of Culloden, as appears from a letter written by him to his brother, John Campbell of Barcaldine, dated at Aberdeen, the 21st April, 1746.[2] He had also served in Flanders. He had evidently engaging personal qualities as appears from the records, from Duncan Bàn Macintyre's elegy to him, and, what is more significant, from the reference to him by Alexander MacDonald (that virulent hater of Campbells and Hanoverians) in the poem entitled "An Airc."[3]

For some time relations between the two men were distinguished by a spirit of compromise. James Stewart acted as a sort of sub-factor, and at first no drastic change occurred in the existing order of things. So much was this the case that at headquarters Glenure became suspected of being a secret Jacobite.[4] This was all the more credible as his mother was a Cameron. At a time when " Pickle " was active, and fears of another rising and foreign invasion were abroad, a Government agent with such sympathies was distinctly undesirable.

4

In order now to consolidate his position Glenure had to display some vigour in his dealings with the late rebels. In January, 1750, James Stewart in Auchindarroch petitions for himself and other tenants that " they are distressed by the Factor, Colin Campbell of Glenure, lately appointed by the Barons, for the rents of the lands possessed by them for the years 1745, 46, 47, and 48, as well as for the current year s rent, 1749, and that they are willing to pay the current and subsequent years' Rents; but with regard to the Bygones they had been compelled to pay them to the late proprietor, Charles Stewart, and his Lady, and on account of their landlord being in the rebellion had their houses burnt, and their cattle and goods mostly carried off and destroyed."[5]

In 1751, prior to the May term, James Stewart was asked to give up the farm of Glenduror, he receiving the farm of Acharn from Campbell of Airds. Campbell of Ballieveolan settled on Glenduror. Although James removed without demonstration, this act of Glenure's rankled in his mind, and when he was in liquor, to which he was evidently increasingly addicted, he was in the habit of uttering threats against Glenure, as men do in those circumstances. Apparently, however, he continued still to apply the surplus rents to the behoof of the Ardsheil family.

The next move was a warning to a number of Jacobite tenants on the Ardsheil estates to remove at Whitsunday, 1752. After Glenure had obtained the Sheriff's authority to evict them, James immediately took up their cause, no doubt from mixed motives—genuine goodness of heart, his responsibility as unacknowledged leader in the district, and the fact that the gradual resetting of the lands to Hanoverian tenants would spell destitution for the family of Ardsheil. On April 3, 1752, he set off for Edinburgh, where he arrived on April 8. Here he presented a memorial to Baron Kennedy, who promised to bring it before the Exchequer Court. But, as there was no meeting of the Baron's Court until June 3, this was useless to stop the Whitsunday evictions. On April 13 Glenure obtained a Precept of Removal against John Colquhoun and others, the Ardsheil tenants. James then presented a Sist or Bill of Suspension to Lord Dun on April 18, and left for home on the following day, where he arrived on the 27th April. At the beginning of May Glenure went to Edinburgh, and on the 5th of May he obtained a refusal of the Sist from Lord Haining. On the 7th of May he left Edinburgh and arrived home on the 9th.

On Monday, May 11, Glenure left home for Fort-William to carry out evictions on Lochiel's estate of Mamore, and on Thursday, May 14, he set out for Appin, where he was to carry out evictions on the following day. Along with him were Donald Kennedy, an Inverary Sheriff-officer; his nephew, Mungo Campbell (a natural son of Glenure's eldest brother, John Campbell of Barcaldine), who was a writer in Edinburgh; and Glenure's servant, John MacKenzie.

The position of the people in Appin was now regarded as desperate. There were strong rumours abroad that Glenure meant to be Laird of Appin. His policy spelled ruin for gentry and common folk alike. It was probably felt that some desperate remedy was necessary. Desperate deeds and the taking of life was not new to a people who had left close on five score of their clan lying on Drumossie Moor only six years before. Theirs had been a noble fight and death on the field of battle. To the cowed survivors remained only the dishonourable work of secret plotters and assassins.

When Glenure was crossing the ferry at Ballachulish, the ferryman, it is said, tried to dissuade him from taking the route he proposed through the wood of Lettermore. But Glenure evidently felt himself safe once he had left the country of his mother's people, the Camerons. On the way he was met by Alexander Stewart of Ballachulish, who

6

conveyed him to the boundary of his estates. Going through the wood of Lettermore the little company was strung out. In front was Donald Kennedy on foot, then came Mungo Campbell, then Glenure's servant, John MacKenzie, and lastly Glenure himself, all on horseback. On entering the wood the servant returned to pick up a coat he had dropped, and thus fell behind Glenure. This was the order of their going when a shot rang out from a bush behind, and Glenure was struck by two bullets entering at his back. Mungo Campbell ran up the hill to see who had shot Glenure, " and saw, at some distance from him, a man with a short dark-coloured coat, and a gun in his hand, going away from him; and; as the deponent came nearer him, he mended his pace, and disappeared by high ground interjected betwixt him and the deponent."[6] This was about 5.30 o'clock in the afternoon and Glenure died about 6.

There was a general belief that many were involved in the plot and that there were more than one at the scene of execution. In his letter, dated Fort William, 23rd May, 1752, Mungo Campbell writes: " From Glenure's words and the situation of the place where I saw one of the villains, there's reason to believe there were more than one on the spot; and circumstances concur in convincing us that there were numbers of Lochabar as well as Appin Potintates in the combination."[7] John Breck MacColl deponed that " two poor women that had come up Glenco were telling, that Glenure was murdered Thursday evening in the wood of Lettermore; and that two people were seen going from the place where he was murdered." Allan Breck Stewart was said to be one of them.[8] Charles Stewart, son of James of the Glen, in his Declaration of 4th June, 1752, stated that on the 14th of May John MacColl had informed him that Glenure had been murdered by a shot and " that there was a man or two seen near the place."[9] Colonel John Crawfurd in a letter, dated at Berwick, 20th May, 1753, quotes an observation of Lord Willoughby of Brook: "That he saw plainly by the Tryal above Twenty five people must have known of the murder, and that only one had been hanged."[10] In a letter from Captain Alexander Campbell to his father, John Campbell of Barcaldine, there is mention of a rumour that it was Allan, James' son, who was with Allan Breck when the murder was committed.[11] Allan's alibi, however, is too good to give any credence to this.[12] These references are important as corroborating, to some extent, the traditional account.

In Campbell and official circles it was generally believed that Allan Breck Stewart was the perpetrator of the deed and that James Stewart of the Glen was accessory and guilty, art or part, of the murder. He and his son, Allan, were arrested on May 16 and taken to Fort William, where they lay until the beginning of September. All possible obstacles were interposed to prevent the prisoner from preparing his defence. By the ordinary procedure the prisoner could have had his trial speeded up and thus have had it heard in the High Court of Edinburgh, where he would have been assured of a more impartial hearing and jury. This he was prevented from doing, and his trial took place at the Circuit Court at Inverary before a packed jury, eleven of whose fifteen members were Campbells. The Duke of Argyll presided as Lord Justice General of Scotland. The trial lasted from September 21 (N.S.) until September 25. The verdict was a foregone conclusion. The Campbells had decided to make a sacrifice and the more influential the better. James Stewart was sufficiently influential to be a proper subject for an "example." His son, Allan, although evidence was equally strong against him, was later dismissed. The evidence led even against the principal was of a sufficiently circumstantial nature. How much more so that against the accessory! At the end of this trial, fittingly described by Sheriff MacPhail as an " impudent mockery,"[13] James Stewart was found guilty and condemned to be hanged. On October 5 he was transferred to Fort William. On November 7 he was removed thence to Ballachulish, where he was executed, protesting his innocence to the last, on November 8. Both tradition and the weight of later legal authority concur in saying that this man of kingly name was innocent.

The question which has exercised generations of people since, many of them first interested in the problem by reading R. L. Stevenson's " Kidnapped " and " Catriona," is, Who fired the shot that killed Colin Campbell of Glenure ? The person generally suspected was Allan Breck Stewart, a son of Donald Stewart (Domhnall mac Iain mhic Alasdair), of Inverchomrie in Rannoch. He had been brought up by James Stewart of the Glen, and appears to have been of a prodigal nature. He joined the British Army, apparently in Colonel Lee's regiment.[14] At the battle of Prestonpans he was taken prisoner, and thereafter served throughout the campaign in the Jacobite army. After Culloden he succeeded in escaping to France, where he enlisted in Ogilvy's Scottish Regiment. He made frequent visits to this country. According to Hugh Stewart's evidence he went to France in 1747, returned to Scotland in December, 1749 ; returned to France in May, 1751, and came back in February, 1752. He probably acted both as intermediary between Ardsheil and his half-brother and as a recruiting officer for the French service. His movements on the day of the murder are highly suspicious, and his subsequent disappearance served in the eyes of many to confirm his guilt. As to the first, although they make him suspect, they do not prove his guilt. As to his disappearance, he had sufficient cause already not to wish to be apprehended —desertion from the British Army, fighting for the Jacobites, serving in the French Army, recruiting therefor on British soil, and conveying rents from the Forfeited Estates to the

9

attainted proprietor.   No wonder Allan Breck did not wish
to be apprehended on a charge of murdering Colin Campbell
of Glenure, against whom, in addition, he had uttered threats.
Against the charge may be placed, for what it is worth, his
own repeated and vehement denial of the accusation, even
after gaining French soil,[15] where he arrived about March,
1753.[16]   It is possible that Allan's conduct and movements
were calculated to divert suspicion from the real author of the
crime, as is suggested by Colonel John Crawfurd in a letter,
dated Fort William, 22nd May, 1752: " I would not have us
being led away with a belief that . . . is the principle person ;
this seems to me calculated to divert our intentions from
objects more in our power, and the way his name has been
mentioned to me by the Stewarts, fully convinces me that
his name and absconding was intended as a peace offering for
the rest of his friends."[17]   Why, if he was willing to incur
the suspicion, he would not have fired the fatal shot himself,
is a question that, for lack of evidence, must remain
unanswered.

It has even been put forward that there was no murder at
all.   This version of the episode is based on a manuscript
account of the career of Robert Mackintosh, who was one of
those who represented James Stewart at his trial.[18]   This
MS. was written in 1840 by a nephew of Robert Mackintosh,
who had been on terms of close friendship with his uncle until
the latter's death in 1805.   According to this MS., Allan
Breck Stewart is said to have made a statement at some period
after 1752 to the effect that he unexpectedly met Glenure in
a wood and that he expostulated with him regarding the
evictions he was about to carry out ; that Glenure did not
answer but tried to seize Allan's gun, which went off in the
ensuing scuffle, shooting Glenure through the body ; that Allan
himself, already a deserter, was fearful of facing a murder
charge, and so escaped from the scene ; and that he did not

know of the proceedings against James Stewart until it was, too late to save his life.[19] This is a most improbable yarn, for the following reasons: (1) There is no such statement by Allan Breck extant; (2) It is in direct conflict with the first-hand testimony of Mungo Campbell, Donald Kennedy, and John MacKenzie; (3) Glenure was shot in the back, a fact testified to by Alexander Campbell, surgeon in Lorn[20]; (4) James and Allan Stewart were arrested on May 16, when Allan Breck was no further away than Koalisnacoan (Caolas nan Con). Allan Breck did not arrive in France until February, 1753, at the earliest. It is therefore highly improbable that he was unaware of the proceedings against James Stewart.

The only other person mentioned as being suspect of the murder was John Dubh Cameron, alias Serjeant Mór.[21] He had served in the French Army and had fought in the Jacobite rising of 1745-6, for which he was outlawed. Thereafter he lived a bandit's life in the Western Highlands, until he was captured in Rannoch. He was executed at Perth on 23rd November, 1753, for the murder of a man who was killed at Braemar during one of his raids. Donald Stewart deponed that, in a conversation with James Stewart on the 15th May, James Stewart said that one serjeant More, alias John Cameron, had been threatening harm to Glenure in France. Donald Stewart also deponed that, to his knowledge, Serjeant Mór had not been in Appin for the past ten years.[22] If James Stewart made this remark, it was probably to divert suspicion from Allan Breck or from the real murderer. John Cameron of Strone deponed that Serjeant Mór Cameron had threatened to shoot Glenure if he met him in the high way.[23] His servant, Ewan Cameron, deponed that he heard Serjeant Mór saying that " he did not care tho' he should be up-sides with " Glenure if he met him.[24] Had the murder occurred in Cameron territory, the facts cited would have been of

11

significance; but, as it is, there is not a shred of evidence to connect Serjeant Mór with the deed.

THE TRADITIONAL ACCOUNT.

The traditional account, here given, is taken from John F. Campbell's MSS. of West Highland Tales, deposited in the National Library. The perpetrator of the deed is said to be Donald Stewart, nephew of Stewart of Ballachulish, and it is said that Stewart of Fasnacloich accompanied him when the murder was committed. According to this account the murder was carefully premeditated and the result of concerted action by the gentry of Appin. So far as known to me this account of the tragedy has only been referred to once before, namely, by Sheriff MacPhail, but he ventures no opinion as to its credibility.[25]

The greater part of the tale was told to John Dewar by Archibald Colquhoun (Gill-easbuig Mac a' Chombaich), who was living in 1865 at Port Appin.[26] Colquhoun had formerly been a farmer in the Airds district, but in his old age he had to give up his farm and become a labourer. In 1865 he was 83 years of age, i.e., he was born in 1782. That means that his grandfather, and possibly even his father, were living close to the scene of the events narrated, and that their account is as likely to be right, in its main thesis, as any. Another of the reciters was Iain Og Mac Sholla or Mac Colla. His mother was a daughter of Donald Stewart, son-in-law to Ballachulish.[27] He was brought up with his grandfather (probably paternal, as the contrary is not stated). His grandfather was close on a hundred years when he died. He had a great store of old lore, and it was from him that Iain Og Mac Sholla learned the old tales he knew. The account which these Appin reciters give of the murder seems to be substantially the same as that at which Andrew Lang hints in his "Historical Mysteries." (The Case of Allan Breck, pp. 74-98).

12

NOTES.

1 The author of the *Supplement* says : " Thus died James Stewart, on the 8th day of November, 1752 aged 57." (*The Trial of James Stewart*, ed. David N. Mackay; 2nd Ed., 1931; App. VIII, p. 341).

2 *Trial*, App. I, p. 303.

3 *Ge toigh leam Cailean Ghlinn Iubhair B'fheàrr leam gum b' iubhar 's nach b'fheàrna* (*Alex. MacDonald* (1924 Edition), p. 258).

4 Lord Glenorchy was constrained to present a Memorial as to his integrity (*Trial*, App. X, p. 345).

5 *Forfeited Estate Papers*, p. 278.

6 Mungo Campbell's deposition (*Trial*, p. 131).

7 *Trial*, App. II, p. 305; *Highland Papers*, Vol. IV, p. 126.

8 *Trial*, p. 182.

9 *Trial*, p. 206.

10 *Trial*, App. XV, p. 362.

11 *Trial*, App. XVIII, p. 384.

12 He was at Innseag with his brother, Charles, and Fasnacloich's daughter (*Trial*, p. 200).

13 *Trans. Gaelic Society Inverness*, XVI, p. 277.

14 Hugh Stewart's deposition; *Trial*, p. 188; elsewhere said to be Lascelles' or Murray's regiment; William Stewart's deposition (*Trial*, p. 178).

15 On the night of Thursday, 14th May, he denied it to Donald Stewart, who said he did not believe him (*Trial*, p. 147). On the afternoon of Saturday, 16th May, he told John Breck MacColl, bouman to Appin in Koalisnacoan (Caolas nan Con), that he had no concern in it (*Ib.*, p. 182). About Monday, 18th of May, he declared, with an oath, to his uncle, Allan Og Cameron, that he had never seen Glenure, dead or alive (*Ib.*, p. 151). In a letter from John Campbell of Achalader to Campbell of Barcaldine, dated Achmore, 5th May, 1753, there is mention of a rumour that Robin Og Drummond or MacGregor had seen Allan Breck in France, that he said it was Allan Beg (perhaps James's son) who had actually committed the murder; and that Breck intended to publish a vindication of himself (*Ib.*, p. 36).

16 *Trial*, App. XV (9), p. 361; App. XVI (1), p. 364.

17 *Trial*, App. XVIII (6), p. 373; although the name has been burnt away, it obviously refers to Allan Breck.

13

[18] Mackintosh appears to have been an able, but erratic and litigious man; cf. *Trial, Biographical Notes*, App. VI, p. 324.

[19] Communication to *Aberdeen Weekly Journal* (14th April, 1916) by Mr A. M. Mackintosh, Nairn; note in *Scottish Hist. Review*, XIII, p. 420, by Mr R. Anderson.

[20] *Trial*, p. 138.

[21] *v.* General Stewart's *Sketches of the Highlanders*, Vol. I, p. 66, and App. H, XXIV-XXV; *Trial, Biographical Notes*, App. VI, pp. 326-7.

[22] *Trial*, p. 147. In his declaration James Stewart stated that Allan Breck had informed him that Serjeant Mór swore he would kill Glenure because of the treatment he gave the tenants on the estate of Mamore, part of Lochiel's estate; and that as soon as he heard of Glenure's murder it occurred to him that Serjeant Mór had done it (*Ib.*, pp. 196-7).

[23] *Trial*, p. 191.

[24] *Trial*, p. 192.

[25] *Highland Papers*, Vol. IV, pp. 123-4.

[26] *v.* MS. *West Highland Tales*, Vol. I, pp. 227-8; for Iain Og Mac Sholla *v.* p. 222.

[27] Is it possible that the alleged murderer was his grandfather? The Donald Stewart cited as a witness at the trial was both nephew and son-in-law of Ballachulish.

CAILEAN GHLINN IUBHAIR.

[MS. *West Highland Tales*, Vol. I, pp. 134-143].

An déidh fairtleachadh air na reubalaich aig Cùil-lodair, chaidh na fearannan aca arfhuntachadh do'n rìgh, agus seanaghail (Chamberlain) a chur a dh'amharc thairis air na fearainn.

B'e duine uasal òg, ris an abairte Cailean Caimbeul Ghlinn Iubhair, a chaidh a chur gu bhith 'na sheanaghal thar fearann Loch Iall an Loch Abar, agus thar fearann Stiùbhartaich na h-Apunn, a bha 'nan reubalaich.

B'e Cailean Ghlinn Iubhair mac do Fhear Bharra-challtuinn agus do nighean Loch Iall. Bha Fear Bharra-challtuinn iar a bhith pòiste dà uair, agus b'e nighean Loch Iall a' bhean mu dheireadh a bha aige. Dh'fhàg a' cheud bean mac, agus b'e Alasdair an t-ainm aige. Dh'eug a' cheud bean, agus phòs Fear Bharra-challtuinn nighean Loch Iall, agus bha mac aice-se, agus b'e Cailean a b'ainm dha. [Bha triuir bhràithrean aig Cailean Ghlinn Iubhair: Alasdair, Daibhidh, agus Donnchadh. Bu leth-bhràthair dhoibh Iain Dubh, ach b'e Iain bu shine, agus b'e an t-oighre].*

Tha sgeul r'a innse uimpe. Bha i an toiseach ro fhaoilidh, agus bha a choltas oirre gun cosgadh i an oighreachd; gus aon latha gun d'thubhairt Fear Bharra-challtuinn rithe, "Faodaidh tusa bhith cho stròdhail is a thogras tu, ach ma chosgas tu na bhios ann de airgead, gheibh Alasdair an oighreachd saor de ainbhfhiach, agus chan fhaigh do mhac-sa ach na bhios an làthair 'na dhéidh sin." Dh'fhàs nighean Loch Iall ro ghrunndail 'na dhéidh sin, agus trath chunnaic i gum b'urrainn i rud a chur mu seach, dh'fhàs i gàbhaidh cruaidh. Agus chuir i mu seach uibhir is a cheannaich Gleann Iubhair

* [ ] indicate additions made to the MS. which have been placed here in their proper context.

do a mac féin, Cailean, agus fhuair e an staoidhle Fear Ghlinn Iubhair.

Bha Cailean Ghlinn Iubhair anns an arm an aghaidh a' Phrionnsa anns na bliadhnaibh 1745 agus '46, agus an déidh do bhlàr Chùil-lodair a bhith seachad, trath rachadh priosanaich a ghlacadh, bha Cailean Ghlinn Iubhair air a chomharrachadh mar fhear a bha ro ghuineideach an aghaidh nan daoine a dh'éirich le Prionnsa Teàrlach. Rachadh e air feadh nam prìosanach, agus trath chitheadh e aon air bhith de na h-oifigich a dh'aithnicheadh e, dh'ainmicheadh e iad. Agus bha e 'na iompaidh air móran de oifigich a' Phrionnsa a bhith air an aithneachadh agus air an cur gu bàs a dh'fhaodadh faighinn as mur bhitheadh Cailean Ghlinn Iubhair air a bhith ann.

Trath chaidh an aghaidh a' Phrionnsa agus nam Fineachan a dh'éirich leis, gus nach robh a chridhe aig aon dhiubh a bhith air am faicinn, chaidh na fearainn aca arfhuntachadh do'n rìgh, agus seanaghail a chur a riaghladh nam fearannan. Agus b'e Cailean Ghlinn Iubhair a chaidh a chur 'na sheanaghal thar fearann Mhic Dhomhnaill Duibh Loch Iall, agus thar fearann Aird Seile, agus nan Stiùbhartach eile anns an Apuinn a dh'éirich leis a' Phrionnsa.· Agus bha Cailean ro shanntach ghionach gu nithean a chur air dòigh gum biodh teachd a stigh gu buannachd dha féin ann.

Bha anns na tìomannan sin feadhainn de Chaimbeulaich aig an robh gabhail mhór fhearainn ann an Gleann Eite, agus, trath bha an aonta aca air teireachdainn, ghabh Fear Fhas na Cloiche am fearann, thar ceann nan Caimbeulach, air son feadhainn de Chloinn Labhruinn ris an robh càirdeas aig na Stiùbhartaich. Agus thubhairt Cailean Ghlinn Iubhair, trath chuala e gun ghabh Fear Fhas na Cloiche fearann a chàirdean, gun tugadh esan air na daoine sin, nach biodh clod de fhearann na h-Apunn seilbhichte le Stiùbhartach, agus nach biodh clod de fhearann Loch Abar seilbhichte le Camshronach. Thog a'

16

chainnt sin gamhlas mór aig muinntir Loch Abar 's na h-Apunn ri Cailean Ghlinn Iubhair, agus bha iad an rùn nam biodag dha.

Bha Teàrlach Stiùbhart Aird Seile air a bhith gleidheadh stòr mine agus nithean eile air son feum na dùthcha, agus b'e leth-bhràthair do'm b'ainm Seumas a bha 'na fhear gleidhidh stòir dha. Agus trath dh'fhalbh Fear Aird Seile do dh'arm a' Phrionnsa, thug e suas an stòr do Sheumas, agus thug e dha gabhail air Gleann Dùrar, agus b'e Seumas a' Ghlinne theirte ris mar fhrith-ainm. Ach trath fhuair Cailean Ghlinn Iubhair bhith 'na sheanaghal air fearann na h-Apunn, dh' arfhuntaich e na bha de spréidh ann an Gleann Dùrar air son an rìgh, agus thug e an stòr bho Sheumas a' Ghlinne. Agus tuilleadh 'na dhéidh sin bha gamhlas mór aig Seumas a' Ghlinne ri Cailean Ghlinn Iubhair.

Chaidh Seumas a' Ghlinne gu mór air an òl an déidh an stòr a bhith iar a thoirt uaithe ; agus trath bhitheadh e air a' mhisg, mar bu bhitheanta a bha e, bhitheadh e a' bagairt gun dèanadh e olc air Cailean Ghlinn Iubhair.

Bha bràthair do Mhac Dhomhnaill Duibh Loch Iall a chomhnaidh ann am baile do 'n ainm am Fasadh Feàrna. Cha d' éirich esan idir leis a' Phrionnsa ; agus bha e toileach uibhir de oighreachd a bhràthar a ghleidheadh dha féin is a b' urrainn dha. Bha anns an am sin fear de Stiùbhartaich Fhas na Cloiche a bha 'na nòtar gu bhith sgrìobhadh bhann, mar ealain. Fhuair Fear an Fhasaidh Fheàrna an nòtar gus còir-bhréige a sgrìobhadh air cuid de na fearannan a bha aig a bhràthair. Bha Alasdair Stiùbhart, an nòtar, 'na dhuine a bha ro shocharach ; gidheadh, bha e suas ris an lagh, agus sgrìobhadh e còir no bann gu pongail. Fhuair Fear an Fhasaidh Fheàrna e gu còir-bhréige a sgrìobhadh, agus sgrìobh Alasdair nòtar còir mar gum biodh Fear an Fhasaidh Fheàrna iar ceannach agus iar pàigheadh earrann de fhearann Loch Iall.

Chnuasaich Cailean Ghlinn Iubhair, gus an d' fhuair e a mach nach robh ach foill-chòir aig Fear an Fhasaidh Fheàrna air na bailtean fearainn a bha e ag agairt. Agus ged a b' e Fear an Fhasaidh Fheàrna mac bhràthair màthar Chailein Ghlinn Iubhair, thug Cailean Ghlinn Iubhair suas do 'n lagh e. Chaidh Fear an Fhasaidh Fheàrna thoirt gu cùirt, agus chaidh fhaotainn a mach gum b' e Alasdair Stiùbhart, an nòtar, a sgrìobh am bann-bréige, agus chaidh Alasdair nòtar a thoirt do Dhùn Eideann a chum deuchainn a chur air.

Bha athair an nòtair 'na sheann duine aig an am; ach gidheadh, chaidh e do Dhùn Eideann a sheasamh cùis a mhic. Cha robh e ceadaichte anns an am sin an éididh Ghàidhealach a chaitheamh, ach chuir athair an nòtair éididh cho Gàidhealach is a dh' fhaodadh e air: còta agus brigis de aodach iar a dhèanamh aig an tigh. Trath chaidh e steach do thigh na cùirte, b' ann a thòisich an luchd lagha ri fochaid air. Thubhairt e, " Is mise athair a' phrìosanaich air a bheil sibh a' cur deuchainn. Am faigh mi cead bruidhinn air a shon?'' Thubhairt an t-àrd bhritheamh gum faigheadh. Thubhairt athair an nòtair, " Tha mi ro bhodhar; is ann le sgrìobhadh as éiginn dhomh bruidhinn ribh.'' . Thug e a mach pàipear as a phòca, agus thug e do 'n luchd lagha e, agus thubhairt e, " So dhuibh pàipear agus leughaibh e.'' Chuir iad am pàipear mu'n cuairt air an luchd lagha, agus leugh fear an déidh fir dhiubh e. Agus thòisich iad ri gàireachdaich air. Thug iad dha a phàipear a rithist, agus thubhairt iad ris gu robh an sin a phàipear aige, nach dèanadh e móran feum dha. Thug athair an nòtair a mach pàipear eile as a phòca, agus thug e dhoibh e gus a leughadh. Chaidh am pàipear a chur mu'n cuairt air an luchd lagha, leugh fear mu seach dhiubh am pàipear, is shìn iad an àirde do 'n Mhorair a bha 'na shuidhe 'sa chathair-chùirt e. Leugh am Morair am pàipear agus thubhairt e ris an luchd lagha, " Faodaidh sibh sgur de bhur gàireachdaich. Tha rudeigin

nach do shaoil sibh an ceann a' bhodaich.'' Chaidh am
pàipear a shìneadh air ais do athair an nòtair agus a ràdh
ris, '' Cha dèan am pàipear sin móran feum dhuit na's mò.''
Thubhairt athair an nòtair, '' Tha pàipear eile agam an so,
nam bitheadh sibh cho maith is amharc air, mur bi e draghail
leibh.'' Thug e dhoibh am pàipear, agus an àite gàireachdaich
air, b' ann a bha iad a' crathadh an cinn ri chéile, agus shìn
iad am pàipear an àirde a dh' ionnsaigh an àrd bhritheimh,
a bha 'na shuidhe an cathair a' bhreitheanais. Sheall am
britheamh air, agus thubhairt e, '' Tha dùil agam féin nach
'eil ann ad mhac ach amadan.'' Thubhairt athair an nòtair,
'' Tha fios nach robh mo mhac-sa ach amaideach bho 'n a
rugadh e. Dhèanadh e mar a rachadh iarraidh air, ach cha
robh e glic. Agus faiceadh sibh-se ciod a ta sibh a' dèanamh.
Ged a tha an lagh a' giùlan gun téid an làmh a thoirt bharr
aon air bhith a nì *forge,* chan 'eil an lagh a' giùlan gun téid
boinne de fhuil a dhòrtadh ; agus ged a bheir sibh an làmh
dheth, chan 'eil e ceadaichte dhuibh boinne de 'n fhuil aige
a dhòrtadh. Do réir lagh Mhaois cha chòir fuil a dhòrtadh
ach air son fola. Ma nì aon goid, is ann a dh' fheumadh e a
cheithir uibhir a phàigheadh air ais. Agus chan 'eil a bhith
a' deanamh foill-chòir ach mar ghoid.'' Dh' éisd am
britheamh ri athair an nòtair gus an do sguir e de labhairt.
Agus an sin thug e breith, gum b' e an dòigh gus an làmh a
thoirt bharr an nòtair, nach faodadh e bann, còir, no nì air
bhith eile a bhuineadh do lagh na rìoghachd, a sgrìobhadh
tuilleadh, air neò nan sgrìobhadh, bha e gu bhith iar a
chrochadh. Fhuair an nòtar dheth air an dòigh sin, ach bha
an dòigh a bha aige gu aran a chosnadh air a mhilleadh air.

Bha mac dìolain do Fhear Aird Seile, leth-bhràthair do
Theàrlach Mór, aig am robh baile fearainn do 'n ainm Beinne-
mhor, ann an Srathaibh Fhaolain. B'e Iain Glas a theirte
ris. Dh' éirich e leis a' Phrionnsa, agus chaidh a mharbhadh
latha blàr Chùil-lodair. Chaidh an spréidh a bha aige

19

arfhuntachadh air son an rìgh, agus chaidh Cailean Ghlinn Iubhair a dhèanamh 'na sheanaghal thar Beinne-mhor mar an ceudna. Bha aig an 'am sin feadhainn anns an Apuinn, a bha a' smaoineachadh gum b' iad féin a b' fheàrr còir air an spréidh a bha iar a bhith aig Iain Glas na an rìgh; agus chaidh iad agus thug iad leotha cuid de 'n chrodh a b' fheàrr a bha anns a' bhaile. Chnuasaich Cailean Ghlinn Iubhair a mach, gus an d' fhuair e fios có iad an fheadhainn a thug air falbh na beathaichean, agus thug e suas do 'n lagh iad. Chaidh na maoir a chur gus an glacadh, agus b' éiginn do na daoine teicheadh, agus an dùthaich fhàgail, air eagal is gun rachadh an crochadh mar mhèirlich; agus cha do phill iad air ais tuilleadh.

Cha dèanadh Cailean Ghlinn Iubhair soileas do aon air bhith de sheann nàisinnich na dùthcha. Thug e aonta trì naoi bliadhna deug air fearann Aird Seile do fhear do 'm b' ainm Pàruig Caimbeul, a bha chomhnaidh anns an Achadh ann am Bràghaid Alban. Agus thubhairt e ri tìom nach biodh gin de shliochd nan Stiùbhartach anns an Apuinn, no gin de shliochd nan Camshronach ann an Loch Abar.

Thog a' chainnt sin gamhlas mór a bhith aig muinntir Loch Abar agus aig muinntir na h-Apunn ri Cailean Ghlinn Iubhair, ionann is gum b' fheàrr leotha e bhith marbh na e bhith beò. Bhitheadh na Camshronaich ann an Loch Abar, agus bhitheadh na Stiùbhartaich anns an Apuinn bitheanta a' bruidhinn mu cho droch-umhaileach is a bha Cailean Ghlinn Iubhair, agus mar a bha e a' rannsachadh a mach agus a' faotainn brath mu na reubalaich, agus 'gan toirt suas do 'n lagh; agus nan leanadh e air a bhith dèanamh mar a bha e a' dèanamh, gum faodadh seann luchd-àiteachadh na tìre an dùthaich fhàgail.

Rinn muinntir na h-Apunn 's Loch Abar suas gun cruinnicheadh cuid de na daoine bu phrionnsalaiche a bha anns an dùthaich, agus gun gabhadh iad comhairle cia mar bu chòir dhoibh a dhèanamh.

Bha cuid de dhaoine anns an dùthaich nach tug suas an airm do 'n rìgh, agus b' iad sin daoine bu mhotha meas anns an dùthaich. Agus shuidhich iad latha gu coinneachadh anns an Apuinn, agus bha gach fear aig an robh gunna gus a toirt leis. B' e an t-àite thagh iad gus coinneachadh aige, àite ris an abrar Lagan Bhlàr an Lochain (Index : Lag Bhlàr an Lochain), far nach cluinnte fuaim nan gunnachan as. Agus mu'n do thòisich iad air feuchainn nan gunnachan, chaidh ionann is bòid a chur air gach fear dhiubh, ge b' e fear aig an robh an gunna a b' fheàrr, gun tugadh e seachad i gu cùis àraid a dhèanamh; agus ge b' e fear a b' fheàrr làmh gus cuimseachadh, gun robh esan gus an gnìomh a dhèanamh.

Choinnich iad air an latha, agus chuir iad deuchainn air na gunnachan, agus b' e gunna a bha aig fear do 'm b' ainm Dùghall Mac Sholla (ris an abairte mar fhrith-ainm Dùghall na Ciabhaig) an gunna a b' fheàrr gu tilgeadh pheileirean. Nan rachadh peileir agus ruagaire a chur innte, thilgeadh i an dithis cho dìreach is nach bitheadh iad tuaiream òirleach o a chéile anns a' chomharra anns an targaid. Agus b' e fear ris an abairte Domhnall mac Dhomhnaill, mac bràthar do Fhear Bhaile Chaolais, am fear a b' fheàrr làmh agus sùil gu cuimseachadh. Chaidh gunna Dhùghaill na Ciabhaig a thoirt do Dhomhnall mac Dhomhnaill, agus bha esan gu dol mar aon gus Cailean Ghlinn Iubhair a thilgeadh. B' e Fear Fhas na Cloiche aon eile a chaidh a thaghadh, a thaobh a bhith maith air a' ghunna, agus chaidh esan a thaghadh air son a' ghnothaich cheudna.

Chaidh Cailean Ghlinn Iubhair aon latha do Loch Abar gu gnothach àraidh a chur an gniomh. Bha fios aig muinntir na h-Apunn roimh làimh gun robh e gu dol ann, agus faraon bha fios aig muinntir Loch Abar air. Agus rinn iad suas gun rachadh an fheadhainn a chaidh a thaghadh air son a' ghnìomha agus gum feitheadh iad fàth air, agus, nam

21

faigheadh iad cothrom air a dhèanamh, gun tilgeadh iad urchair air Cailean agus gum marbhadh iad .e. Chaidh feadhainn a chur air freiceadan ann an Loch Abar le gunnaichean gus a mharbhadh, agus fòs aig Baile Chaolais. B' ann am fagus do 'n Leitir Mhóir a bha an luchd feall-fhalach a bha 'ga fheitheamh air taobh Baile Chaolais. [Chaidh Fear Fhas na Cloiche agus Domhnall mac Dhomhnaill, mac bràthar do Fhear Bhaile Chaolais, agus dh' fheith iad aig creig mhóir dhuibh a ta am fagus do 'n Leitir Mhóir; agus gheàrr iad meur bharr preas beithe a bha an sin, oir is gum faigheadh iad an gunnaichean a leigeadh air a' phreas, agus gum bitheadh iad féin am falach].

Trath chuir Cailean air a ghnothach ann an Loch Abar, dh' fhalbh e gu dol dachaidh, agus bha duine-uasal eile maille ris, agus bha gille leis. Trath thàinig iad chun an àite far an robh am fear gamhlais am falach, bha an duine-uasal eile a' marcachd ri taobh Chailein, agus bha e eadar Cailean 's am fear feall-fhalach. Air an aobhar sin cha d' fhuair am fear feall-fhalach fàth air an urchair a losgadh air Cailean, air eagal an duine-uasal eile a mharbhadh. Air an aobhar sin fhuair Cailean sàbhailte seach am fear sin.

Trath ràinig Cailean air adhart gu ruige an t-aiseag, thubhairt am Portair Cam ris, " Tha dùil agam, a Chailein, gur fheàrr dhuit fanail agus do leaba a ghabhail còmhla rium féin a nochd. Tha eagal orm gu bheil feadhainn aig a bheil droch rùn riut air an rathad air thoiseach ort." Thubhairt Cailean, " Chan 'eil eagal air bhith orm a nis bho 'n a fhuair mi á dùthaich mo mhàthar, ach chan 'eil eagal orm air an taobh eile de Loch Lìobhunn." Thubhairt am Portair Cam ris, " Is e mo chomhairle dhuit co dhiùbh, thu a dh' fhanail agam-sa a nochd, air neò, mur fan, thu a dhol a mach Gleann an Fhiodhaich agus dol sìos Gleann Dùrar." Ach thubhairt Cailean, " Chan 'eil eagal air bhith orm a nis bho 'n a fhuair mi sàbhailte thar a' chaolas." Agus dh' fhalbh e féin agus a ghille agus iad a' marcachd air muin eich. Trath ràinig iad creag mhór dhubh a ta am fagus do 'n Leitir Mhóir, bha Cailean pailt air thoiseach air a' ghille; bha an luchd feall-fhalach bràigh na creige le an gunnachan; loisg fear dhiubh urchair air Cailean, agus bhuail an dà pheileir e air a' chliabhaich, beagan na b' ìsle na an asgailt; agus thubhairt Cailean ri a ghille, " Tha dùil agam gu bheil mi iar mo thilgeadh." Chaidh e air adhart astar beag, agus an sin thuit e bharr an eich. [Sheall . . . an rathad a thàinig an urchair, agus chunnaic e dithis dhaoine, agus gunnaichean fada aca, agus chunnaic e gun robh ciù air cùl cinn an fhir a loisg an urchair].

Ghabh an gille eagal, agus chuir e an spuir ris an each aige gu maith, agus ghabh e air adhart gus an do ràinig e tigh Sheumais Stiùbhairt, mac dìolain Fhear Aird Sëile, ris an abairte Seumas a' Ghlinne. Agus bhuail an gille aig an dorus aige. Bha Seumas a' Ghlinne iar a bhith an latha sin, e féin agus a ghille, ag obair air cur eòrna. Bha an talamh iar a bhith bog, agus bha casan Sheumais a' Ghlinne salach le créidh an àirde thar na glùinean; agus trath chuala e gille Chailein Ghlinn Iubhair aig an dorus, chaidh e do 'n t-seòmar, agus chunnaic gille Chailein Ghlinn Iubhair e, ach cha do leig e air gum faca, ach dh' fharraid e an robh e stigh. Agus chaidh a ràitinn ris nach robh. Agus dh' innis an gille gun deach a mhaighstir a mharbhadh shuas am fagus do 'n Leitir Mhóir. Agus, trath fhuair Seumas a' Ghlinne aodach glan a chur air, thàinig e an làthair gille Chailein Ghlinn Iubhair. Dh' innis an gille do Sheumas a' Ghlinne gun deach Cailean Ghlinn Iubhair a thilgeadh, agus dh' iarr e air Seumas a' Ghlinne e a dhol leis gus Cailean Ghlinn Iubhair a thogail. Bha Seumas toileach dol ann, ach bhac a bhean e, agus cha deach e ann.

Bha feirg mhór air càirdean Chailein Ghlinn Iubhair mu dhéighinn bàs Chailein, agus fòs bha fearg mór air a' chuid

mhóir de na h-uaislean Caimbeulach mu a dhéighinn. Bha
iad a' rannsachadh a mach feadh na dùthcha a dh' fheuchainn
am faigheadh iad brath air feadhainn air bhith a bha an
droch rùn do Chailean.

Thachair gum b' àbhaist do Sheumas a' Ghlinne a bhith
bitheanta anns an tigh-òsda; agus, trath bhiodh misg air,
bhitheadh e daonnan a' bruidhinn air Cailean Ghlinn
Iubhair, agus 'ga chàineadh air son a bhith cho guineideach
an aghaidh an fheadhainn a dh' éirich leis a' Phrionnsa, agus
gu h-àraidh mu 'n chron a rinn Cailean air Seumas a' Ghlinne
e féin; agus bhitheadh e bitheanta a' maoidheadh, nam
faigheadh e fàth air Cailean, gun dèanadh e olc an àite uile.

Bha aon uair a bha Seumas a' Ghlinne ann an cuideachd,
agus bha cuid de fheadhainn an sin a bha càirdeil ri Cailean
Ghlinn Iubhair, agus bho'n a bha iad ag òl co dhiùbh, thug
iad fainear gun òladh iad air slàinte Chailein Ghlinn Iubhair.
Thubhairt Seumas a' Ghlinne, " Chan òl mise i." Thubhairt
aon de 'n chuideachd ris, "Agus ciod a dhèanadh tu ma tà?"
Thubhairt Seumas a' Ghlinne, " Dhèanadh, a chasan a
tharruing, nam bitheadh e air a' chroich."

Chaidh aire a thoirt do 'n chainnt sin aig an am, agus a
ghleidheadh air chuimhne; agus trath bha airgead air a
thairgse do aon air bhith a bheireadh brath air aon air bhith
de 'n fheadhainn a bha an droch rùn do Chailean Ghlinn
Iubhair, chaidh brath a thoirt air cainnt Sheumais a' Ghlinne.
Agus chaidh na maoir a chur air, agus a ghlacadh, agus a
thoirt do phrìosan Inbhir Aoradh.

Chaidh faraon umhail a chur gun robh làmh aig Fear Fhas-
na Cloiche ann am murtadh Chailein Ghlinn Iubhair. Agus
chaidh brath a thoirt do 'n t-Siorram gun deach Fear Fhas-
na Cloiche fhaicinn a' dol ris a' mhonadh, bràigh Fhas na
Cloiche, an latha roimh an oidhche air an deach Cailean
Ghlinn Iubhair a mharbhadh, agus e armaichte le gunna.
Agus chaidh fear do 'm b' ainm Domhnall Mac an t-Saoir,

24

a bha chomhnaidh ann an Inbhir Pholla, a shumanadh 'na aghaidh.

Chaidh Domhnall Mac an t-Saoir a thoirt an làthair an t-Siorraim agus a cheasnachadh; agus chaidh fharraid dheth am faca e Fear Fhas na Cloiche fo armaibh air an latha air an deach Cailean Ghlinn Iubhair a mharbhadh. Thubhairt Domhnall Mac an t-Saoir nach faca, agus cha robh tuilleadh fhianaisean aca air a' phuing sin, agus b' éiginn dhoibh sgur de dheuchainn Fhir Fhas na Cloiche, agus esan a leigeadh mu sgaoil.

Tamull na dhéidh sin bha Fear Fhas na Cloiche a' dol seach Inbhir Pholla. Chunnaic e Domhnall Mac an t-Saoir ag obair, agus ghlaodh e ris, "Thig an so; tha mi los bruidhinn riut." Agus ghlaodh e ri companach Dhomhnaill Mhic an t-Saoir, "Thig thusa a nìos cuideachd, a Dhomhnaill Mhic Gille-Mhìcheil, oir is gun cluinn thu an nì a théid a ràdh." Chaidh Domhnall Mac an t-Saoir agus Domhnall Mac Gille-Mhìcheil far an robh Fear Fhas na Cloiche. Thubhairt Fear Fhas na Cloiche ri Domhnall Mac an t-Saoir, "Tha mi móran 'nad chomain air son nam mionnan-eithich a thug thu aig Inbhir Aoradh gus mise a thèarnadh." Thubhairt Domhnall Mac an t-Saoir, "A mhic an riabhaich, a bheil thu ag ràdh gun tug mise na mionnan-eithich air do shon?" Thubhairt Fear Fhas na Cloiche, "Innis dhomh ma tà, a Dhomhnaill, ciod e an dòigh a ta agad air thu féin a shaoradh?" Thubhairt Domhnall Mac an t-Saoir, "Chaidh fharraid dhiom am faca mi Fear Fhas na Cloiche air an latha roimh an oidhche air an deach Cailean Ghlinn Iubhair a thilgeadh a' dol ris a' mhonadh agus e fo armaibh. Thubhairt mise nach faca. Chan fhaca mise agad ach aon ghunna, agus, tha fios agad féin, ghabhadh e dithis a dhèanamh airm no armaibh." Thubhairt Fear Fhas na Cloiche, "Ro cheart, tha thu 'gad shaoradh féin air an dòigh sin."

Chaidh Seumas a thoirt air beulaibh na cùirte aig Inbhir Aoradh, agus mhair an deuchainn a chaidh a chur air ré thrì làithean. Ach ré na tìoma sin cha d' fhuair iad nì air bhith 'na aghaidh leis am b' urrainn iad a dhìteadh.

Mu dheireadh chaidh fear de mhuinntir Ghlinn Dùrar, do 'm b' ainm Iain Breac MacSholla, a thoirt a stigh 'na fhianais 'na aghaidh; agus chaidh esan a cheasnachadh mu dhéighinn na facail a chuala e Seumas a' Ghlinne ag ràdh an aghaidh Chailein Ghlinn Iubhair.

Bha Iain Breac Mac Sholla iar a bhith 'na dhìlleachdan, agus bha e iar a bhith ré tìom fhada 'na dhìol-déiric ann an tigh Sheumais a' Ghlinne. B' e Seumas a' Ghlinne a dh' àraich e bho 'n a bha e 'na phàisde, agus bha e iar a bhith bitheanta ann an cuideachd Sheumais a' Ghlinne trath bhitheadh Seumas air a' mhisg, agus chuala e móran de chainnt Sheumais.

Chan 'eil fios co dhiùbh a chaidh no nach deach duais a ghealltainn do Iain Breac Mac Sholla air son fianaïs a thoirt an aghaidh Sheumais a' Ghlinne, ach bha e ag innse a h-uile nì a chuala e Seumas ag ràdh an aghaidh Chailein Ghlinn Iubhair, agus mu 'n droch rùn a bha aige dha. Trath dh' innis Iain Breac Mac Sholla gach nì a b'urrainn dha a chuimhneachadh an aghaidh Sheumais a' Ghlinne, chaidh a leigeadh a mach á seòmar na cùirte. An déidh dha dol a mach á ionad na cùirte, bha e féin agus a bhean a' bruidhinn mu 'n fhianais a thug e. Dh' fharraid a bhean dheth, "An d' innis thu dhoibh gun cuala thu Seumas Stiùbhart aon uair ag ràdh gun rachadh e trì mìle air a ghlùinean gus coileach-dubh a dhèanamh de Chailean Ghlinn Iubhair?" Thubhairt Iain Breac Mac Sholla, " Ma tà, cha do chuimhnich mi." Thubhairt a bhean, " Ma tà, is fheàrr dhuit pilltinn fhathast agus innse." Phill Iain Breac a rithist do thigh na cùirte agus thubhairt e, " Rinn mi dìochuimhne. Cha do chuimhnich mi innse dhuibh gun cuala mise Seumas

Stiùbhart, agus misg air, ag ràdh gun rachadh e trì mìle air a ghlùinean gus coileach-dubh a dhèanamh de Chailean Ghlinn Iubhair.''

An sin thug am britheamh breith air Seumas Stiùbhart, gun robh e gu bhith iar a chrochadh aig Cnap a' Chaolais, agus gu bhith air fhàgail an crochadh ris a' chroich; agus b' e sin féin a chaidh a dhèanamh.

[An déidh do Sheumas a' Ghlinne a bhith iar a dhìteadh, agus e 'na laighe anns a' phrìosan, bha duilichinn mhór air Domhnall mac Dhomhnaill mu dhéighinn e féin, a rinn an dòibheart, a bhith saor, agus gun umhail a bhith air a chur air, agus an duine a bha neochiontach a bhith air a dhìteadh gu bhith air a chrochadh 'na àite-san. Agus bha e los e féin a thoirt suas do 'n lagh, gu fhulang air a shon féin, agus an duine neochiontach a leigeadh saor. Ach chruinnich pàirtidh de uaislean na dùthcha d'a ionnsaigh, agus chomhairlich iad uaithe sin e. Chuir iad an céill ris gun do ghabh Ailean Breac Stiùbhart air féin a cheana gum b' e am fear a mharbh Cailean Ghlinn Iubhair; gidheadh, nach do rinn sin maith air bhith do Sheumas a' Ghlinne. Agus ged a bheireadh Domhnall mac Dhomhnaill e féin suas gum b'e an ciontach, nach dèanadh e ach nì a bha gu dona a roimhe a dhèanamh na bu mhiosa na mar a bha e: ged a bheireadh Domhnall mac Dhomhnaill e féin suas nach saoradh sin Seumas a' Ghlinne o 'n chroich, ach gum bitheadh iad le chéile iar an crochadh, agus a' chuid eile de uaislean na dùthcha air am fògradh as an rìoghachd].

Bha fear de mhuinntir na dùthcha ris an abairte Ailean Breac Stiùbhart. Ghabh esan air féin gum b' e am fear a mharbh Cailean Ghlinn Iubhair. Bha e ré tamuill 'ga fhalach féin mu Cheann Loch Bige agus mu Ghleann Lìomhann. Ri tìom fhuair e teicheadh, agus chaidh e do 'n Fhraing; agus chuir e fios air ais gum b' esan a mharbh Cailean Ghlinn Iubhair, agus ged a chaidh Seumas a' Ghlinne a chrochadh air a shon, gun robh e neochiontach dheth. Agus b' e sin bu naidheachd ré tìom fhada.

27

An déidh bàis Dhiùc Ghill-easbuig, bha a charaid, Iain, 'na Dhiùc. Bha Diùc Iain ro mheasail aig an rìgh,' agus rinn an rìgh e 'na àrd riaghladair air a h-uile caisteal a bha ann an Albainn; agus bhitheadh e a' dol uair anns a' bhliadhna d' am faicinn, a shealltainn cia mar a bha iad air an gleidheadh an òrdugh.

Aig an am sin bha fear gòrach, ris an abairte Mac a Phì a' chuthaich, a' teachd corr uair o Loch Abar do 'n Apuinn; agus chaidh cuideigin de mhuinntir Bhaile Chaolais agus leag iad a' chroich air an robh Seumas a' Ghlinne air a chrochadh, agus chuir iad air Mac a Phì a' chuthaich gum b' esan a leag i; agus ghabh Mac a Phì ris, agus thubhairt e gum b' e.

Aig an am sin bha Diùc Iain Earra Ghàidheal a' dol a chuairt a choimhead nan caisteal, agus bha eagal air Iain Buidhe, Tighearna Bhaile Chaolais, trath thigeadh Diùc Earra Ghàidheal, gum biodh fearg mhór air o'n aobhar gun deach croich Sheumais a' Ghlinne a leagadh. Agus thug e òrdugh do mhuinntir Ard nan Saor, an oidhche a bhitheadh Diùc Earra Ghàidheal aig an àite sin, iad a chur gille gu luath a dh' innse dha-san.

Trath ràinig an Diùc Ard nan Saor, chaidh gille a chur a thoirt fios do Fhear Bhaile Chaolais, agus bha Fear Bhaile Chaolais a' feitheamh aig Caolas Mhic Phàruig trath thàinig an Diùc air adhart. Chuir e fàilte air an Diùc. Thubhairt an Diùc ris, '' Chan 'eil mi 'gad aithneachadh.'' Thubhairt Fear Bhaile Chaolais, '' Is e Iain Stiùbhart m' ainm. Tha oighreachd bheag agam an so aig Baile Chaolais; agus bu chomain leam nam fanadh sibh agus oidhche a chur seachad leam.'' Thubhairt an Diùc, '' Tha, ar leam, gu bheil mi ag cuimhneachadh gum faca mi a roimhe thu.''

Chaidh an Diùc le Iain Buidhe do thigh Bhaile Chaolais.

Bha ceithir de choin gheala aig an Diùc leis. Chaidh iad-san a chur do thigh dhoibh féin. Fhuair an Diùc aoigheachd mhaith ann am Baile Chaolais, agus an ath latha thubhairt an Diùc ri Fear Bhaile Chaolais, "A bheil nì air bhith a ta 'nam chomas-sa a dhèanamh air do shon as àill leat mi a dhèanamh?" Thubhairt Iain Buidhe Bhaile Chaolais, "Ma tà, tha ban-choimhearsnach agam agus bu ro mhaith leam gum faighinn cead a cur air falbh." Thubhairt an Diùc, "Nach leat féin Baile Chaolais, agus nach fhaod thu do thoil féin a dhèanamh air t' fhearann féin?" Thubhairt Iain Buidhe, "Chan fhaod. Tha aon bhan-choimhearsnach agam nach faod mi a chur as an fhearann gun bhur toil-se : is e sin a' chroich air an deach Seumas a' Ghlinne a chrochadh, agus tha i a' cur móran farrain orm." Thubhairt an Diùc, "Na gabh ort nì air bhith, ach cur as i; cha b'ann le m'thoil-sa gun robh i riamh ann. Rinn mi na b' urrainn mi 'na aghaidh. Ach rinn am fear a bha 'na Dhiùc anns an am sin mar a thogradh e féin." Bha an sin cead a' chroich a chur air falbh.

Dh' fhàg an Diùc Baile Chaolais an latha sin, agus chaidh e do Ard Chatain.

Bha ceithir de choin gheala aig an Diùc leis, agus, trath bha iad aig Baile Chaolais, fhuair iad biadhtachd mhaith o Bhean Bhaile Chaolais. Ach cha d' fhuair iad ach biadh bochd aig Ard Chatain, agus bhris iad a mach as an tigh anns an robh iad, agus dh' fhalbh iad air an ais do Bhaile Chaolais a rithist.

Anns a' mhaduinn, trath dh' éirich gille an Diùc, bha na coin air falbh. Agus chaidh an gille agus dh' innis e do 'n Diùc gun d' fhàg na coin e. Dh' fharraid an Diùc, "Ciod am biadh a fhuair iad an raoir?" Dh' innis an gille. Dh' fharraid an Diùc, "Ciod am biadh a fhuair iad aig Baile Chaolais?" Dh' innis an gille. Thubhairt an Diùc, "Faodaidh tusa, ma tà, dol do Bhaile Chaolais a dh'iarraidh nan con, agus gheibh thu an sin iad. Tha e coltach leam gun tachair gille Fhir Bhaile Chaolais ort a' teachd leis na coin. Agus abair ris e a theachd air adhart, còmhla riut-sa agus ris na coin, gu ruige Inbhir Aoradh."

Dh' fhalbh an Diùc dhachaidh, agus phill a ghille a dh' iarraidh nan con. Agus, trath bha e a' dol suas taobh na Linne Seilich, thachair gille Bhaile Chaolais e aig an Luirgeanach, agus na coin aige. Agus dh' iarr gille an Diùc air gille Fhir Bhaile Chaolais e a dh' fhalbh leis gu Inbhir Aoradh. Chaidh gille Fhir Bhaile Chaolais maille ri gille an Diùc gu ruige Inbhir Aoradh; agus thug an Diùc sine* 'na làimh dha, ach cha d'fhuair neach eile fios ciod a fhuair e.

Bha an Diùc agus a' Bhan-Diùc còmhla aon latha, agus dh' fharraid a' Bhan-Diùc, " Càite an d' fhuair thu an fhaoileachd a b' fheàrr a fhuair thu, trath bha thu air do thurus?" Thubhairt an Diùc, " Ma tà, fhuair aig Baile Chaolais, bho Iain Buidhe Stiùbhart." Thubhairt a' Bhan-Diùc, " Ma tà, tha thusa glé mhurrach air breaban a chur air a bhròig." Bha anns an am sin fearann aig an Diùc eadar Baile Chaolais agus Gleann Comhann, agus thug an Diùc còir air an fhearann ris an abrar Lurg Mhic Cailein, agus o sin suas gu ruige an t-àite ris an abrar Port Eachainn gu e bhith na dhubhairidh do Bhean Bhaile Chaolais.

Tìom fhada an déidh bàis Chailein Ghlinn Iubhair, chaidh Alasdair Caimbeul, Fear Bharra-challtuinn, agus Domhnall mac Dhomhnaill agus gillean leotha do mhonadh Raithneach a shealg fhiadh. B' e gunna fada Bhaile Chaolais, ris an abairte an t-Slinneanach mar ainm, a bha aig Domhnall mac Dhomhnaill, mac bràthar Fhir Bhaile Chaolais. Bha Domhnall mac Dhomhnaill agus Fear Bharra-challtuinn ré an latha a' falbh troimh mhonadh Raithneach gun fhiadh fhaicinn. Trath bha e teann air an fheasgar, rinn iad suidhe ann an lagan a bha an sin, agus thòisich iad ri ithe bìdh a bha aca leotha. Bha iad ag amharc mu 'n cuairt dhoibh, agus thug iad an aire do rud cosmhail ri preas air bearradh os an ceann. Bha iad ré tamuill an teagamh co dhiùbh a b'e preas seilich no cròic féidh a bha ann. Mu dheireadh leag Domhnall

* MS. sinne.

30

mac Dhomhnaill an t-Slinneanach air sorchan, agus a beul-dois ris a' chròic a bha iad a' faicinn, agus thubhairt e ris a' ghille aige, " Dèan fead." Rinn an gille fead, ach cha do charaich a' chròic. Thubhairt Domhnall mac Dhomhnaill, " Dèan fead as cruaidhe." Rinn an gille fead bu chruaidhe, agus dh' éirich fiadh gu h-àrd air a' bhearradh. Chum Domhnall mac Dhomhnaill an gunna ris. Thubhairt Fear Bharra-challtuinn, "Amadain, a bheil dùil agad gun dèan thu dheth aig an astar sin ?" Loisg Domhnall mac Dhomhnaill an urchair, agus mharbh e am fiadh. Thubhairt Fear Bharra-challtuinn, " Cha do shaoil mi féin gun dèanadh gunna 'sam bith an tùrn aig an astar."

Chaidh iad gu ruige far an robh am fiadh, agus bha e buailte cùl an t-slinnein, agus bha am peileir agus an ruagaire mar an dà leud do a chéile. Sheall Fear Bharra-challtuinn air an dòigh iar an deach am fiadh a bhualadh, agus thubhairt e, " Is e sin dìreach a' cheart dòigh air an deach Cailean, mo bhràthair-sa, a bhualadh ; agus is meallta mise, air neò is e a' cheart gunna a rinn an gnìomh, co air bhith làmh anns an robh i." Thubhairt Domhnall mac Dhomhnaill, "A bheil dùil agad gur e mise a mharbh do bhràthair ?" Thubhairt Fear Bharra-challtuinn, " Chan 'eil, ach tha mi ag ràdh gur e sin an dòigh air an do bhuail an dà pheileir e." Thubhairt Domhnall mac Dhomhnaill, " Nan saoilinn gun robh thu ag eudachadh rium-sa gum bu mhi a mharbh do bhràthair, cha rachadh tusa dhachaidh." Thubhairt Fear Bharra-challtuinn, " U chan 'eil, ach tha mi a' toirt aire gum b' e sin an dòigh air an do bhuail an dà pheileir e." Thog a' chainnt sin fuarachd eadar an dithis, agus chaidh gach fear dhiubh a rathad féin dhachaidh.

Chaidh ainm a thogail gun robh e cunnartach an gunna do 'm b' ainm an t-Slinneanach a ghleidheadh ann an tigh, bho 'n aobhar gun rachadh ge b' e tigh anns am bitheadh i ri theine. Chaidh a gleidheadh ann an tigh beag, a bha air a

31

thogail air a son féin, ré tamuill; agus chaidh a cur do dh'
àiteigin mu thuath 'na dhéidh sin. Ach cha robh eagal air
na daoine aig an robh i 'ga gleidheadh mu thuath gun cuireadh
i an tigh ri theine. Agus chaidh Domhnall mac Dhomhnaill chun na mara,
agus cha do phill e tuilleadh. Leàn mac a bha aige mar an
ceudna air a' mhuir gus an d' eug e.

Agus an déidh bàis Dhomhnaill mhic Dhomhnaill agus a
mhic, chaidh an sin innse gum b' e Domhnall mac Dhomhnaill,
mac bràthar Fear Bhaile Chaolais, a mharbh Cailean Ghlinn
Iubhair.

A' Chrìoch.

TRANSLATION.

After the rebels had failed at Culloden, their estates were forfeited to the king, and factors were appointed to supervise the estates.

It was a young gentleman, called Colin Campbell of Glenure, who was appointed to be factor on the estate of Lochiel in Lochaber, and on the estate of the Stewarts of Appin, who had been rebels.

Colin of Glenure was the son of the Laird of Barcaldine and Lochiel's daughter. The Laird of Barcaldine had been married twice, and Lochiel's daughter was his second wife. The first wife left a son whose name was Alexander.[1] The first wife died, and the Laird of Barcaldine married Lochiel's daughter, and she had a son and Colin was his name. [Colin of Glenure had three brothers: Alexander, David, and Duncan. John Dubh was half-brother to them, but John was the eldest and he was the heir].[2]

There is a tale told of her. She was at first extremely hospitable, and she looked like to dissipate the estate, until one day the Laird of Barcaldine said to her, " You may be as prodigal as you like, but if you spend all the money there is, Alexander will get the estate free from debt and your son will only get what is left thereafter." Lochiel's daughter grew very economical after that, and when she saw that she could save somewhat, she became terribly stingy. And she saved as much as bought Glenure for her own son, Colin, and he received the style Laird of Glenure.

Colin of Glenure was in the army against the Prince in the years 1745 and 46, and after the battle of Culloden[3] was over, when prisoners were made, Colin of Glenure was distinguished as a man who was most vengeful against the men who had risen with Prince Charles. He was wont to go among the prisoners, and, whenever he saw any of the officers whom he knew, he named them. And he was a means of many of the Prince's officers being recognised and put to death, who might have escaped if it had not been for Colin of Glenure.

When matters had gone against the Prince and the Clans who had risen with him, so that none of them dared show themselves, their estates were forfeited to the king, and factors were appointed to administer these estates. And it was Colin of Glenure who was appointed factor on the estate of Cameron of Lochiel, and on the estate of Ardsheil and those other Stewarts in Appin who had risen with the Prince.[4] And Colin was most greedy and covetous to arrange matters so that a profit should accrue to himself.

There were in those times some Campbells who had a large holding in Glen Etive, and, when their lease had expired, the Laird of Fasnacloich leased the land over the heads of the Campbells for some MacLarens who were related to the Stewarts. And Colin of Glenure said, when he heard that the Laird of Fasnacloich had taken his friends' land, that he would deal with those men so that not a clod of the land of Appin would be possessed by a Stewart nor a clod of the land of Lochaber possessed by a Cameron. This talk caused the people of Lochaber and Appin to bear great malice against Colin of Glenure, and they were at daggers drawn with him.

Charles Stewart of Ardsheil had been keeping a store of meal and other things for the use of the country, and it was a half-brother called James who was his store-keeper. When the Laird of Ardsheil left for the army of the Prince, he gave up the store to James, and he gave him a lease of Glen Duror, and he was called James of the Glen as by-name. But when Colin of Glenure got to be factor on the estates of Appin, he confiscated all the cattle in Glen Duror for the king, and he took the store from James of the Glen.[5] And ever after that James of the Glen bore a great grudge against Colin of Glenure.

James of the Glen took greatly to drink after the store had been taken from him; and, when he was drunk, as he very often was, he used to threaten that he would do Colin of Glenure harm.

Cameron of Lochiel had a brother dwelling in a farm called Fassiefern.[6] He did not rise at all with the Prince; and he desired to keep for himself as much of his brother's inheritance as he could. There was at that time one of the Stewarts of Fasnacloich, who was a notary for writing deeds by profession. The Laird of Fassiefern got the notary to write a false charter for some of the lands which his brother had. Alexander Stewart, the notary, was a very simple man. Nevertheless he was skilled in the law and he could write a charter or bond correctly. The Laird of Fassiefern got him to write a false charter, and Alexander the notary wrote a charter as if the Laird of Fassiefern had bought and paid for a portion of Lochiel's lands.

Colin of Glenure probed until he discovered that the Laird of Fassiefern had only a forged right to the farms which he claimed, and, although the Laird of Fassiefern was Colin of Glenure's cousin, Colin of Glenure delivered him into the hands of the law. The Laird of Fassiefern was tried, and it was discovered that it was Alexander Stewart, the notary, who had forged the bond, and Alexander, the notary, was taken to Edinburgh to be tried.

The notary's father was an old man at the time; nevertheless, he went to Edinburgh to appear in his son's defence. It was not permitted at that time to wear the Highland garb, but the notary's father clad himself in a dress as Highland as he could: a coat and trousers of home-spun cloth. When he entered the court-house the lawyers began to jeer at him. He said, " I am the father of the prisoner whom you are

35

trying. May I obtain permission to speak for him?'' The chief judge said that he might. The notary's father said, '' I am very deaf; it is by writing I must speak to you.'' He took a paper out of his pocket, gave it to the lawyers and said, '' Take this paper and read it.'' The lawyers sent the paper round, and one after another of them read it. And they began to laugh over it. They gave him his paper back, and they said to him that there he had his paper, that it would not do him much good. The notary's father took another paper out of his pocket and he gave it to them to read. The paper was sent round the lawyers, each read the paper in turn, and they handed it up to the law-lord who was presiding over the court. The law-lord read the paper, and said to the lawyers, '' You may stop laughing. There is something that you did not think in the old man's head.'' The paper was handed back to the notary's father and he was told, '' That paper will not do you much good either.'' The notary's father said, '' I have another paper here, if you would be so good as to read it, if it be not tiresome for you.'' He gave them the paper, and instead of laughing over it, they were shaking their heads at one another, and they handed the paper up to the chief judge, who was sitting in the seat of judgment. The judge looked at it and said, '' I believe myself that your son is nothing but a fool.'' The notary's father said, '' It is well known that my son was foolish from birth. He would do as he was asked, but he was not wise. And see ye to it what ye do. Although the law is to the effect that the hand shall be cut off anyone who is guilty of forgery,[7] the law does not provide for a drop of his blood being shed; and though you cut off his hand, you are not allowed to shed a drop of his blood. According to the law of Moses it is not right to shed blood save for blood. If one committed theft, he had to make restitution four-fold. And forgery is only as theft.'' The judge listened to the notary's father until he had finished speaking. Then he gave judgment that the way to cut off the notary's hand was that he should be henceforth debarred from writing a bond, charter or anything else that pertained to the law of the kingdom, or if he did write them he was to be hanged. The notary was acquitted in this wise, but his means of earning a livelihood was destroyed for him.

There was a natural son of the Laird of Ardsheil, a half-brother of Charles Mór, who had a farm called Benmore in Strath Fillan. He was called John Glas.[8] He rose with the Prince, and he was killed at the battle of Culloden. His cattle were confiscated for the king, and Colin of Glenure was likewise appointed factor over Benmore. There were at that time some in Appin who thought that they had a better right to the cattle which John Glas had had than the king ;[9] and they went and carried off some of the best cattle that were on the farm. Colin probed until he got information of those who had taken the beasts away, and he turned the matter over to the law. Sheriff-officers were set to capture them, and the men were forced to flee and to leave the country, for fear they should be hanged as thieves ;[10] and they returned no more.

Colin of Glenure would show no consideration for any of the old natives of the country. He gave a lease of three-nineteens of the land of Ardsheil to a man called Patrick Campbell,[11] who lived in Achadh in Breadalbane. And he said that through time none of the race of the Stewarts would be in Appin, and none of the race of the Camerons in Lochaber.

That talk caused the people of Lochaber and the people of Appin to bear great malice against Colin of Glenure, so that they would rather he were dead than alive. The Camerons in Lochaber and the Stewarts in Appin were constantly talking of how suspicious Colin of Glenure was, and how he was hunting out and obtaining information regarding the rebels, and delivering them over to the law, and that if he continued to do as he was doing the old inhabitants of the land might leave the country.

The people of Appin and Lochaber arranged that some of the most princely men in the country should meet and should take counsel as to what was best for them to do.

There were some men in the country who had not surrendered their arms to the king, and these were the men most respected in the country. They fixed a day on which they should meet in Appin, and every man who had a gun was to take it with him. The place they selected to meet at was a place called Lagan Bhlàr an Lochain, from which the sound of the guns could not be heard. Before they began to try the guns, what amounted to an oath was imposed on every one of them, that whoever had the best gun should hand it over for a certain purpose; and whoever was the best shot was to do the deed.[12]

They met on the appointed day, and they tested the guns, and it was a gun belonging to a man called Dugald MacColl[13] (known by the by-name of Dugald of the Locks) that was the best gun for firing bullets. If a bullet and a chaser were put into it, it would fire the two so straight that they would not be an inch from each other in the mark in the target. And it was a man called Donald son of Donald,* brother's son to the Laird of Ballachulish,[14] who was the man with the best hand and eye for marksmanship. Dugald of the Locks' gun was given to Donald Stewart, and he was to go with the object of killing Colin of Glenure. The Laird of Fasna-cloich[15] was another who was chosen on account of his skill with the gun, and he was chosen for the same business.

Colin of Glenure went one day to Lochaber to execute a certain commission.[16] The people of Appin knew beforehand that he was going there, and the people of Lochaber likewise

* Hereafter called Donald Stewart.

knew of it. They arranged that those who had been chosen for the deed should go and waylay him, and if they got an opportunity that they should shoot at Colin and kill him. Some were stationed in Lochaber with guns to kill him, and also at Ballachulish. It was near Lettermore that the ambushers who were waiting for him on the side of Ballachulish were. [The Laird of Fasnacloich and Donald Stewart, brother's son to the Laird of Ballachulish, went and waited at a large, black rock, which is near Lettermore ; and they cut a branch from a birch bush that was there, so that they could rest their guns on the bush and themselves remain hidden].

When Colin had completed his business in Lochaber, he set out for home, and there was another gentleman with him and there was a servant with him.[17] When they came to the place where the enemy was lurking,[18] the other gentleman was riding by Colin's side, and he was between Colin and the ambusher. On that account the ambusher did not get an opportunity of shooting at Colin, for fear of killing the (other) gentleman. On that account Colin got safely past that man.

When Colin reached the ferry, the Portair Cam (the Squint or One-eyed Ferryman)[19] said to him, "I think, Colin, you had better stay and put up at my house to-night. I am afraid that some who wish you ill are on the road in front of you." Colin said, "I am in nowise afraid now that I have won out of my mother's country, but I am not afraid on the other side of Loch Leven." The Portair Cam said to him, "My advice to you, at all events, is to stay with me to-night, or if you do not, to go out Gleann an Fhiodhaich and to go down Glen Duror." But Colin said, "I am in nowise afraid now that I have got safely across the ferry." And he and his servant left riding on horseback. When they reached a large, black rock that is near Lettermore, Colin was fully ahead of his servant ; the ambushers were on the

39

rock above with their guns; one of them fired a shot at Colin, and the two bullets struck him in the breast, a little below the armpit; and Colin said to his servant, " I think I have been shot."[20] He went forward a short distance and then he fell from the horse.[21] [. . . looked in the direction from which the shot came, and he saw two men with long guns, and he saw that there was a cue on the back of the head of the man who had fired the shot].[22]

The servant took fright, and he plied his horse well with the spur, and proceeded until he reached the house of James Stewart, natural son of the Laird of Ardsheil, who was called James of the Glen. And the servant knocked at his door. James of the Glen had been that day, himself and his servant, working at sowing barley. The ground had been soft, and James of the Glen's legs were dirty with clay to above the knees; and when he heard Colin of Glenure's servant at the door, he retired to his chamber, and Colin of Glenure's servant saw him, but he did not disclose that he had seen him, but he enquired if he was at home. And he was told that he was not.[23] And the servant told that his master had been killed up near Lettermore. And when James had put on a clean suit of clothes he came into the presence of Colin of Glenure's servant. The servant told James of the Glen that Colin of Glenure had been shot, and he asked James of the Glen to go with him to remove Colin of Glenure. James was willing to go, but his wife restrained him and he did not go.[24]

Colin of Glenure's friends were greatly enraged over Colin's death, and likewise the greater part of the Campbell gentry were greatly enraged over it. They were hunting out throughout the country to see if they could obtain information of any persons whatsoever who wished Colin ill.

It happened that James of the Glen was in the habit of being frequently in the change-house; and, when he was drunk, he was constantly talking about Colin of Glenure, and dispraising him for being so vengeful against those who had risen with the Prince, and particularly of the wrong that Colin had done to James of the Glen himself; and he was constantly threatening that, if he got an opportunity, he would repay Colin evil with evil.

There was one time that James of the Glen was in company, and there were some there who were friendly to Colin of Glenure, and, since they were drinking in any case, 't occurred to them to drink to the health of Colin of Glenure. James of the Glen said, " I will not drink it." One of the company said to him, "And what would you do then?" James of the Glen said, " I would draw down his feet, if he were on the gibbet."[25]

Notice was taken of that conversation at the time, and it was borne in mind; and when money was offered to anyone who would give information against any of those who wished Colin of Glenure ill, information was given regarding James of the Glen's words. The Sheriff-officers were set on him, and he was captured and taken to the prison of Inverary.[26]

Suspicion was likewise laid on the Laird of Fasnacloich that he had a hand in the murder of Colin of Glenure.[27] And information was given to the Sheriff that the Laird of Fasnacloich had been seen taking to the hills above Fasnacloich on the day before the night on which Colin of Glenure had been killed, and that he was armed with a gun. And a man called Donald Macintyre, who lived in Inbhir Pholla, was summoned against him.

Donald Macintyre was brought before the Sheriff and questioned; and he was asked if he had seen the Laird of Fasnacloich under arms on the day on which Colin of Glenure was killed. Donald Macintyre said that he had not, and they had no more witnesses on that point, and they had to stop trying the Laird of Fasnacloich, and to set him at liberty.

Some time after that the Laird of Fasnacloich was going past Inbhir Pholla. He saw Donald Macintyre working, and he called to him, "Come here; I wish to speak to you." And he called to Donald Macintyre's companion, "You come down too, Donald Carmichael, that you may hear what will be said." Donald Macintyre and Donald Carmichael went to where the Laird of Fasnacloich was. The Laird of Fasnacloich said to Donald Macintyre, "I am much obliged to you for having perjured yourself at Inverary to save me." Donald Macintyre said, "Devil take you, do you say that I perjured myself for your sake?" The Laird of Fasnacloich said, "Tell me then, Donald, how do you clear yourself?" Donald Macintyre said, "I was asked if I had seen the Laird of Fasnacloich, on the day before the night on which Colin of Glenure was killed, taking to the hills under arms. I said that I had not. I saw only one gun in your possession and you know yourself it would take two to make ' arms.' " The Laird of Fasnacloich said, "Quite right, you clear yourself in that way."

James was brought before the court at Inverary, and his trial lasted three days.[28]   But during that time they found nothing whatsoever against him with which they could condemn him.

At last a native of Glen Duror, called John Breck MacColl,[29] was introduced as a witness against him; and he was questioned regarding the words he had heard James of the Glen utter against Colin of Glenure.

John Breck MacColl was an orphan, and he had been for a long time maintained in James of the Glen's household through James' charity. It was James of the Glen who had reared him since he was a child, and he had been constantly in James of the Glen's company when James was drunk, and he had heard much of James' talk.

It is not known whether or not a reward had been promised to John Breck MacColl to bear witness against James of the Glen,[30] but he told everything that he had heard James of the Glen utter against Colin of Glenure, and of the ill-will he bore to him. When John Breck MacColl had told everything he could remember against James of the Glen, he was let out of the court-room. When he had gone out of the place of trial, he and his wife were talking of the evidence he had given. His wife enquired of him, "Did you tell them that you once heard James Stewart saying that he would go three miles on his knees to make a blackcock of Colin of Glenure?"[31] John Breck MacColl said, "Indeed I forgot." His wife said, "Well then, you had better return again and tell it." John Breck returned again to the court-house and he said, "I forgot something. I forgot to tell you that I heard James Stewart saying once when he was drunk that he would go three miles on his knees to make a blackcock of Colin of Glenure."

The judge then passed judgment on James Stewart, that he was to be hanged at Cnap a' Chaolais, and to be left hanging on the gallows, and that was what was done.

After James of the Glen had been condemned, and while he was lying in prison, Donald Stewart was smitten with great grief for that he himself, who had committed the misdeed, was free and that he was held in no suspicion, and that the man who was innocent was condemned to be hanged in his stead. And he intended to deliver himself over to justice, to suffer it for himself, and to let the innocent man go free. But a party of the gentry of the country gathered to meet him and they counselled him from that course. They pointed out to him that Allan Breck Stewart had already confessed to being the man who had killed Colin of Glenure; nevertheless that that had not done James of the Glen any good. And, though Donald Stewart should give himself up as being guilty, that

43

it would only make a matter that was bad already worse than it was: although Donald Stewart should give himself up that that would not save James of the Glen from the gibbet, but that they would both be hanged, and that the remaining gentry of the country would be banished from the kingdom].[32]

There was one of the natives of the country who was called Allan Breck Stewart. He took on himself the responsibility for having killed Colin of Glenure.[33] He was for a while lurking about Ceann Loch Bige and Glen Lyon. Eventually he managed to escape, and he went to France; and he sent word back that it was he who had killed Colin of Glenure, and, though James of the Glen had been hanged for it, that he was innocent of it. And for a long time that was the general belief.

After the death of Duke Archibald, his friend (relative), John, was Duke.[34] Duke John was much esteemed by the king, and the king made him chief governor of every castle in Scotland; and he used to go once every year to inspect them, to see in what order they were preserved.

At that time there was a simpleton, called the mad Macphee, who came occasionally from Lochaber to Appin. One of the natives of Ballachulish went and threw down the gibbet on which James of the Glen had been hanged, and they put the blame for having thrown it down on the mad Macphee; and Macphee admitted it, and said that he had done it.[35]

At that time Duke John of Argyll was making his round inspecting the castles, and John Buidhe (Yellow), Laird of Ballachulish,[36] was afraid that when the Duke of Argyll came, he would be greatly enraged because James of the Glen's gibbet had been thrown down. And he gave orders to the people of Ardersier to send a messenger swiftly to him to tell him the night on which the Duke of Argyll was at that place.

When the Duke reached Ardersier a messenger was sent to inform the Laird of Ballachulish, and the Laird of

Ballachulish was waiting at Caolas Mhic Phàruig when the Duke approached. He greeted the Duke. The Duke said to him, " I do not recognise you." The Laird of Ballachulish said, " John Stewart is my name. I have a small estate here at Ballachulish; and I should consider it an honour if you would stay and spend a night with me." The Duke said, " I think I remember now that I saw you before."

The Duke went with John Buidhe to Ballachulish House. The Duke had four white hounds with him. They were put in a house for themselves. The Duke got good hospitality in Ballachulish, and the next day the Duke said to the Laird of Ballachulish, " Is there anything that is in my power to do for you that you wish me to do?" John Buidhe of Ballachulish said, " Indeed I have a neighbour and I wish I could get permission to remove her." The Duke said, " Is Ballachulish not your own, and may you not do as you please on your own land?" John Buidhe said, " No. I have one neighbour whom I may not remove from the land without your permission; that is the gibbet on which James of the Glen was hanged, and it gives me much offence." The Duke said, " Say nothing, but remove it. It was not with my consent that it was ever there. I did what I could against it. But the one who was Duke at that time did as he pleased himself." That was permission to remove the gibbet.

The Duke left Ballachulish on that day, and he went to Ardchattan.

The Duke had four white hounds with him, and, when they were at Ballachulish, they got good provant from the Lady of Ballachulish. But they got but poor food at Ardchattan, and they broke out of the house in which they were, and they made for Ballachulish again.

In the morning, when the Duke's servant arose, the hounds were away. The lad went and told the Duke that the hounds had left him. The Duke enquired, " What food did they get last night ?'' His servant told him. The Duke enquired, " What food did they get at Ballachulish ?'' His servant told him. The Duke said, " You may go, then, to Ballachulish to seek the hounds, and you will get them there. I think it likely that you will meet the Laird of Ballachulish's servant coming with the hounds. And tell him to come with you and with the hounds to Inverary.''

The Duke went home, and his servant returned to seek the hounds. And when he was going up by the side of Loch Linnhe, Ballachulish's servant met him at the Luirgeanach with the hounds. The Duke's servant asked the Laird of Ballachulish's servant to go with him to Inverary. The Laird of Ballachulish's servant went with the Duke's servant to Inverary ; and the Duke placed a teat (?) in his hand, but no one else discovered what he had got.

The Duke and the Duchess were together one day, and the Duchess enquired, " Where did you get the best hospitality that you got while you were on your journey ?'' The Duke said, " It was at Ballachulish from John Buidhe Stewart.'' The Duchess said, " Well, you are very able to put a heel to his shoe.'' At that time the Duke had land between Ballachulish and Glencoe, and the Duke gave the rights of the land called Lurg Mhic Cailein and from there up to the place called Port Eachainn to be a dowry to the Lady of Ballachulish.

A long time after the death of Colin of Glenure, Alexander Campbell, Laird of Barcaldine,[37] and Donald Stewart went with gillies to the moor of Rannoch to hunt deer. It was Ballachulish's long gun, called the Slinneanach, which Donald Stewart, brother's son to the Laird of Ballachulish, had with him. Donald Stewart and the Laird of Barcaldine were, throughout the day, traversing the moor of Rannoch without seeing a deer. When it was close upon evening they sat them down in a hollow and began to eat food which they

46

had with them. They were looking about them, and they noticed a thing like a bush on the brow of a hill above them. They were for some time in doubt whether it was a clump of willows or the antlers of a deer. At length, Donald Stewart laid the Slinneanach on a rest with its muzzle to the antlers which they were seeing, and he said to his servant, " Whistle !" The gillie whistled, but the antlers did not move. Donald Stewart said, " Whistle louder !" The gillie whistled louder, and a deer started up high on the brow of the hill. Donald Stewart aimed his gun at it. The Laird of Barcaldine said, " You fool, do you think you can manage it at that distance ?" Donald Stewart fired the shot and he killed the deer. The Laird of Barcaldine said, " I did not think that any gun would do the trick at the distance."

They went to where the deer was, and it had been struck behind the shoulder, and the bullet and the chaser were only about two breadths from each other. The Laird of Barcaldine looked at the way in which the deer had been struck, and he said, " That is exactly the way in which Colin, my brother, was struck ; and I am much mistaken if that is not the very gun which did the deed, whatever the hand which held it." Donald Stewart said, " Do you think that it was I who killed your brother ?" The Laird of Barcaldine said, " No. But I am saying that that is the way in which the two bullets struck him." Donald Stewart said, " If I thought that you were accusing me of having killed your brother, you would not go home." The Laird of Barcaldine said, " Oh no, I am not, but I notice that that is the way in which the two bullets struck him." That talk occasioned a coolness between the two, and each of them went his own way home.

A rumour arose that it was dangerous to keep the gun called the Slinneanach in a house, because any house in which it would be would take fire. For a while it was kept in a small house which had been built for itself ; and it was sent

47

to some place in the north after that. But the people who were keeping it in the north were not afraid that it would set the house on fire.[38]

Donald Stewart went to sea, and he returned no more. His son likewise followed the sea until he died.

And after the death of Donald Stewart and his son, it was then told that it was Donald Stewart, brother's son to the Laird of Ballachulish, who had killed Colin of Glenure.

The End.

[MS. *West Highland Tales*, Vol. I, pp. 231-233].

Duille 42.   Bha Iain Glas Stiùbhart na Beinne-móire iar a
mharbhadh aig Cùil-lodair.   Chaidh cuid de Chlann
Sholla Bheinne-beithir agus thug iad air falbh cuid de 'n
spréidh, air eagal is gum bitheadh iad air an arfhuntachadh le muinntir an rìgh.
Duille 43.   Bha cuid de fhearann Loch Iall aig Fear an
Fhasaidh Fheàrna air ghabhaltas.   Agus bha e toileach
dòigh fheuchainn gus còir fhaotainn air fearann a
bhràthar nach aithnichte nach bu chòir laghail a bha
ann.   Agus fhuair e Teàrlach Stiùbhart, fear do 'm b'
ealain a bhith 'na nòtar, a sgrìobhadh bann bhréige dha
air fearann a bha air ghabhaltas aige.
Duille 45.   Chaidh Cailean Caimbeul, mac Bharra-challtuinn,
ris an abairte Cailean Ghlinn Iubhair, a chur 'na
sheanaghal air an fhearann a bha iar a bhith aig na
reubalaich.

Bha gamhlas mór aig an fheadhainn a bha iar a bhith
'nan reubalaich ri Cailean Ghlinn Iubhair, bho 'n aobhar
gum b'e a bhrath Fear Cheann Loch Mùideart agus
bràthair Mhic Raghnaill na Ceapaich.   Trath fhuair
Duille 46.   Cailean Ghlinn Iubhair a bhith 'na sheanaghal,
bha e ro shanntach agus cruaidh air an fheadhainn a bha
iar a bhith 'nan reubalaich.   Fhuair e fios gum b' iad
Clann Sholla Bheinne-beithir a thug air falbh an spréidh
á Beinne-mhor.   Thug e suas do 'n lagh iad agus b'éiginn
dhoibh-san teicheadh agus an dùthaich fhàgail.   Mharbh
Duille 47.   Cailean Ghlinn Iubhair Bean Channdalaich,
chionn gun deach i eadar e agus reubal a bha e a' dol a
ghlacadh.   A bharrachd air sin thilg Cailean fear eile de

na reubail a bha a' teicheadh uaithe. Mar an ceudna
fhuair Cailean Ghlinn Iubhair brath gun robh Seumas a'
Ghlinne a' toirt na bha de theachd a mach an Aird Seile,
a bharrachd air na phàigheadh am màl, do theaghlach
Theàrlaich Stiùbhairt, gu e bhith aca air son beathachadh.
Agus thug e Aird Seile bho Sheumas a' Ghlinne, agus
thug e aonta thrì naoi bliadhna deug air Aird Seile do
fhear de mhuinntir Bhràghaid Alban do'm b'ainm Pàruig
Caimbeul, ris an abairte Pàruig an Achaidh. Agus
fhuair Cailean Ghlinn Iubhair brath, trath bha e a' togail
nam màl an Loch Abar, nach robh ach còir-bhréige aig
Fear an Fhasaidh Fheàrna air na bailtean de fhearann
Loch Iall a bha e ag agairt. Thug e a' chùis suas do 'n
lagh. Chaidh a' chùis an aghaidh Fear an Fhasaidh
Fheàrna aig an lagh agus b' éiginn do Fhear an Fhasaidh
Fheàrna innse gum b'e Teàrlach an Nòtar a sgrìobh a'
chòir-bhréige. Chaidh Teàrlach an Nòtar a thoirt do
Dhùn Eideann agus deuchainn a chur air aig mòd; agus
chaidh breith a thoirt air nach faodadh e bhith 'na nòtar
tuilleadh.

Duille 54. Dh' fheuch muinntir Loch Abar is na h-Apunn
am faigheadh iad gun dèanadh Cailean Ghlinn Iubhair
bàidh riutha, ach cha dèanadh Cailean Ghlinn Iubhair
sin. Chaidh Fear Challairt a dh' fheuch am faigheadh
e fàth air Cailean a mharbhadh le urchair gunna. Ach
cha d' fhuair aig an am sin.

Duille 55. Rinn muinntir na h-Apunn agus Loch Abar suas
gum marbhadh iad Cailean Ghlinn Iubhair. Chaidh iad
gu Lag Bhlàr an Lochain a chur deuchainn air na
gunnaichean. B' e gunna Dhùghaill na Ciabhaig gunna
a b' fheàrr, agus b' e Domhnall mac Dhomhnaill, mac
bràthar do Fhear Bhaile Chaolais, cuspair a b'fheàrr.

Duille 57. Chaidh Cailean Ghlinn Iubhair agus Mungo
Caimbeul, mac a bhràthar, do Loch Abar, agus chaidh an

50

fheadhainn a bha gus an gnìomh mharbhaidh a dhèanamh
am feall-fhalach a' feitheamh ris.
(Bho Ghill-easbuig Mac a' Chombaich, am Port Apunn).

Bha feadhainn ann an dà àite an Loch Abar, agus
feadhainn ann an àite 'san Apuinn gus Cailean Ghlinn
Iubhair a mharbhadh. Fhuair e seach an dà àite ann
Duille 59. an Loch Abar, ach chaidh a mharbhadh am fagus
do'n Leitir Mhóir le Domhnall mac Dhomhnaill, agus bha
Fear Fhas na Cloiche leis trath rinn se e.
(Bho Ghill-easbuig Mac a' Chombaich,
agus bho I. Mac Coinnich, 'san Làrfhaich).

Duille 62. Chaidh amharus a leagadh air Seumas a' Ghlinne,
gun robh làmh aige ann am marbhadh Chailein Ghlinn
Iubhair. Chaidh a dhèanamh 'na phrìosanach. Chaidh
Duille 65. a thoirt do Inbhir (Aora) agus deuchainn a chur
air. Ged nach robh e ciontach, chaidh a dhìteadh.
(Iain Og Mac Sholla &
Gilleasbuig Mac a' Chombaich, Pt. Apn.
I. Mac Coinnich &).

Duille 67. Bha duilichinn mhór air Domhnall mac
Dhomhnaill an neochiontach a bhith iar a dhìteadh, agus
esan, a bha ciontach, a bhith bàn-saor. Bha e toileach
e féin a thabhairt suas agus innse gum b' esan e féin a
mharbh Cailean Ghlinn Iubhair. Ach chum a' chuid
eile de uaislean na dùthcha grabadh air, air eagal gun
tugadh e sgrios air an dùthaich.
(Bho I. Mac Coinnich 'san Làrfhaich).

Chaidh croich a chur suas aig Cnap a' Chaolais, agus
chaidh Seumas a' Ghlinne a chrochadh rithe, agus bha e
suas ris a' chroich ré tìom fhada. Bha móran farrain air
muinntir na dùthcha a bhith a' faicinn an caraid ris a'
chroich.

51

Duille 69.   Bha cùram nan caisteal anns a' Ghàidhealtachd air Diùc Earra Ghàidheal aig an am.   Trath bha e a' dol a chuairt a choimhead nan caisteal, bha e a' dol dachaidh tre Bhaile Chaolais.   Choinnich Fear Bhaile Chaolais an Diùc aig Caolas Mhic Phàruig.   Chuir se chun a thighe e.   Thug e aoigheachd oidhche dha, agus thug an Diùc dha cead corp Sheumais a' Ghlinne a thiodhlacadh agus a' chroich a chur air falbh.

(Bho Iain Og Mac Sholla
agus bho Ghill-easbuig Mac a' Chombaich).

Chaidh Domhnall mac Dhomhnaill agus Alasdair, mac Bharra-challtuinn, do mhonadh Raithneach a shealg fhiadh.   Mharbh Domhnall mac Dhomhnaill fiadh, agus thug Alasdair a' Bharra-challtuinn aire gun do chuir gunna Dhomhnaill mhic Dhomhnaill na peileirean ri taobh a chéile, mar a bha na peileirean leis an deach Cailean Ghlinn Iubhair a mharbhadh.   Chaidh amharus a chur gum b' i an t-Slinneanach leis an deach Cailean a mharbhadh, agus chuir muinntir Bhaile Chaolais an gunna sin as an rathad.

(Bho I. Mac Coinnich 'san Làrfhaich).

A' Chrìoch.

52

Page 42. John Glas Stewart of Benmore was killed at Culloden. Some of the Clan Coll (Sholla) of Beinn a' Bheithir went and took away part of the cattle, for fear they should be confiscated by the king's party.

Page 43. The Laird of Fassiefern had a lease of part of Lochiel's estate. He was willing to find a way to obtain a right over his brother's estate, which could not be recognised from a legal claim. He got Charles Stewart, who was by profession a notary, to write a false bond for him of land which he had on lease.

Page 45. Colin Campbell, son of Barcaldine, called Colin of Glenure, was made factor on the lands which the rebels had had.

Those who had been rebels bore great ill-will against Colin of Glenure because it was he who had betrayed the Laird of Kinlochmoidart and MacDonald of Keppoch's

Page 46. brother. When Colin of Glenure got to be factor he was most covetous and hard in his dealings with those who had been rebels. He obtained information that it was the Clan Coll (Sholla) of Beinn a' Bheithir who had taken away the cattle from Benmore. He handed them over to the law, and they were forced to flee and to leave the country. Colin of Glenure killed the Lady of

Page 47. Canndalach because she came between him and a rebel he was about to capture. Moreover, Colin shot another of the rebels who was fleeing from him. Likewise Colin of Glenure discovered that James of the Glen was giving the surplus of the rents of Ardsheil to Charles Stewart's family that they might have it to support them. So he took Ardsheil from James of the Glen, and he gave a lease of three-nineteens of Ardsheil to a man from

Breadalbane named Patrick Campbell, who was called Patrick of Achadh. And Colin of Glenure obtained information when he was collecting the rents in Lochaber, that the Laird of Fassiefern had only a forged right to the tacks of Lochiel which he claimed. He gave the matter into the hands of the law. The case at law went against the Laird of Fassiefern, and the Laird of Fassiefern was forced to tell that it was Charles the Notary who had written the forged charter. Charles the Notary was brought to Edinburgh and tried at court of law; and he was debarred further from being a notary.

Page 54. The people of Lochaber tried to get Colin of Glenure to show them kindness, but Colin of Glenure would not do that. The Laird of Callart went to see if he would get an opportunity to kill Colin with a gun. But he did not get an opportunity at that time.

Page 55. The people of Appin and Lochaber decided to kill Colin of Glenure. They went to Lag Bhlàr an Lochain to test the guns. Dugald of the Locks' gun was the best, and. Donald Stewart, brother's son to the Laird of Ballachulish, was the best marksman.

Page 57. Colin of Glenure and Mungo Campbell, his brother's son, went to Lochaber, and those who were to commit the murderous deed went to await him to waylay him.

(From Archibald Colquhoun, in Port Appin).

There were people in two places in Lochaber, and some in a place in Appin to kill Colin of Glenure. He Page 59. got past the two places in Lochaber, but he was killed in the vicinity of Lettermore by Donald Stewart, and the Laird of Fasnacloich was with him when he did it.

(From Archibald Colquhoun,
and from J. MacKenzie, in Laroch).

Page 62. Suspicion was laid on James of the Glen that he had a hand in the killing of Colin of Glenure. He was
Page 65. made a prisoner. He was taken to Inverary and tried. Although he was not guilty, he was condemned.
(John Og MacColl &
Archibald Colquhoun, Pt. Apn.
J. MacKenzie &).

Page 67. Donald Stewart was smitten with great grief that the innocent man had been condemned, and that he, who was guilty, went scot-free. He wished to give himself up and tell that it was he himself who had killed Colin of Glenure. But the other gentlemen of the country prevented him, for fear he should bring destruction on the country.
(From J. MacKenzie in Laroch).

A gibbet was erected at Cnap a' Chaolais, and James of the Glen was hanged on it, and he was hanging on the gibbet for a long time. It gave the people of the country much offence to be seeing their friend on the gibbet.
Page 69. The Duke of Argyll had charge of the castles in the Highlands at the time. When he was making his round inspecting the castles he was going home through Ballachulish. The Laird of Ballachulish met the Duke at Caolas Mhic Phàruig. He invited him to his house. He gave him hospitality for the night, and the Duke gave him permission to bury James of the Glen's body and to put the gibbet away.
(From John Og MacColl
and from Archibald Colquhoun).

Donald Stewart and Alexander, Barcaldine's son, went to the moor of Rannoch to hunt deer. Donald Stewart killed a deer, and Alexander of Barcaldine noticed that Donald Stewart's gun placed the bullets beside each other like the bullets with which Colin of Glenure had been killed. It came to be suspected that it was with the Slinneanach that Colin had been killed, and the Ballachulish household put that gun out of the way.

(From J. MacKenzie in Laroch).

The End.

NOTES.

1 This should be John (born *c.* 1700, *ob.* 1777), son of Patrick Campbell of Barcaldine and Agnes Campbell of Kilmun. He was a factor on some of the forfeited estates. He sold his estate to his half-brother, Duncan. Alexander was a full brother of Colin, and was an officer in the army. In a note to the tale John is given as heir and is called Iain Dubh.

2 The issue of Patrick Campbell of Barcaldine and Lucy, 12th child of Sir Ewen Cameron by his second wife, Isabel, eldest daughter of Sir Lachlan Maclean of Duart, was : (1) Colin of Glenure; (2) Donald, a surgeon in the Royal Navy; (3) Alexander, an officer in the army; (4) Duncan, who succeeded his father in the estates; (5) Archibald, an officer in the army; (6) Robert, a merchant; (7) Allan, a general officer; (8) Isabella, who married Campbell of Achalader; (9) Mary, who married MacDougall of MacDougall; (10) Annabella, who married Campbell of Melfort; (11) Jane, who married Campbell of Edinchip. (MacKenzie, *History of Clan Cameron*).

3 Glenure was not present at Culloden as appears from his letter, dated at Aberdeen, 21st April, 1746. (*Trial*, App. I, 3, p. 303).

4 His appointment as Factor dates from Feb. 23, 1749.

5 Campbell of Ballieveolan got James's stock of cattle in Glenduror (*v.* his 1st declaration, *Trial*, p. 195).

6 This was John Cameron of Fassiefern, second son of John Cameron, 18th of Lochiel, by his wife, Isabella, sister of Sir Duncan Campbell of Lochnell. He was thus grandson of Sir Ewen (17th of Lochiel), and brother of Donald, the " Gentle Lochiel,' 19th of Lochiel.

On August 7, 1753, he was charged with forgery. It was said that Charles Stewart had forged some of the papers in question. Among the witnesses examined was an aged solicitor in Appin, Alexander Stewart (perhaps Charles Stewart's father, *v.* Lang, *Historical Mysteries*, p. 86), who attested that he had written and witnessed some of the deeds as early as 1713. The Chief of Appin deponed that Charles Stewart, writer in Banavie, accused now of forging a bond of debt, had really written and witnessed it. Fassiefern was, in 1755, sentenced to ten years' banishment, which he passed at Alnwick, and Charles Stewart was deprived of his office of Notary Public (*v.* Lang, *The Companions of Pickle*, pp. 160-172; *v.* also *Memorial for Fassiefern, Highland Papers*, Vol. III, pp. 40-51).

57

The case was later in point of time than the Appin case, but for some considerable time there had been determined efforts to "uproot" Fassiefern. In the *Index to the Tales* Alasdair Stiùbhart is called, correctly, Teàrlach Stiùbhart.

7 For dismemberment of hand (and tongue) in cases of forgery *v. Commentaries on the Law of Scotland respecting Crimes,* Third Edition, Vol. I, 1829, p. 137, and *Principles of the Criminal Law of Scotland,* by Archibald Allison, Edinburgh, 1832, p. 428. Formerly, though the punishment was not expressly laid down by statute, all gross cases of forgery were capital at common law, and in cases of less moment, an arbitrary punishment was inflicted. The punishment of death was first of all restricted 1 Will. IV, c. 66, and 2 and 3 Will. IV, c. 123, and by 1 Vict., c. 84, totally abolished in cases of forgery—transportation for life or for a term of years being substituted. See Bell's *Dictionary on Digest of the Law of Scotland,* Edinburgh, 1861, p. 393. (I owe this and the reference on cattle-stealing to the kindness of Dr John Cameron).

8 John Glas Stewart was the second son of John Stewart of Acharn, who was the eldest son of Alexander Stewart, second son of Duncan Stewart, 2nd of Ardsheil. He acquired the estate of Benmore in Perthshire and was killed at Culloden. (*The Stewarts of Appin,* by John H. J. Stewart and Lieut.-Colonel Duncan Stewart, p. 131).

9 According to the *Index to the Tales* these were Clann Mhic Sholla Beinn a' Bheithir.

10 For cattle-stealing see *Commentaries on the Law of Scotland respecting Crimes,* by David Hume, Third Edition, Vol. I, 1829, p. 88, where sentence of death was pronounced as late as 1827.

11 Patrick Campbell : This appears to be Pàra Mór Aird Seile, who composed *Thogainn fonn air lorg an fhéidh* and *Màiri Og (An t-Oranaiche,* p. 127). He distinguished himself at the Battle of Minden (1759). He was 6 feet 4 inches in height, and was possessed of great strength. The inscription on his tombstone in the Craigs burying-ground, Fort William, is as follows :—
" Sacred to the memory of Captain Peter Campbell, late of the 42nd Regiment, who died on the XIII of December, MDCCCXVI, aged eighty-three years. A true Highlander, a sincere friend, and the best deer-stalker of his day." (*Celtic Monthly,* Vol. V, p. 209).

12 There is not the faintest rumour of such an incident in the official records of the trial, but in a letter from John Campbell

(presumably of Levenside) to John Campbell of Barcaldine, dated Inverary, 2nd Sept., 1752, there is a significant allusion : . . . " Torry precognosed by the man told me he had nothing to say on Either Syde. *I much wish some thing coud come out of the Shooting Match.* Rankine the herd knows his fishing road wanted a hook but has a Devill for now he tells he seed Allan Breck fix a hook to it and Catch fish. . ."(*Trial*, App. XVIII 26, p. 386). The reference can hardly be to the attempts to " uproot " Fassiefern. In the Winter (*i.e.*, later than the above letter) of 1752 Cameron of Glen Nevis swore to Sheriff Douglas that he had been fired at on his way home from Fort William, wishing thereby to implicate Fassiefern. " Notwithstanding of the strictest inquiry that he could make it came to nothing and though there was people, close to the place he pretended he was fired at watching a Corps, there was none of them heard a shott, so that all he gained by this adventure was that every person belived that he perjured himself, beside it can be proven that a few nights after the *shoting match* he travelled home all alone under night." (*Highland Papers*, Vol. III, pp. 49-50).

13 James Stewart had two servants of the name Dougal MacColl, but it was probably a common name in the district. Although cited in the trial as MacColls, they do not seem to have been MacColls at all. At least the writer of the tales writes, for the most part, Mac Sholla and Clan Sholla. In Campbell's MS. *Tales* they are said to be descended from a certain Solla, who lived near Oban, and eventually settled at Innseag in Appin. (MS. *West Highland Tales*, Vol. I, p. 212). They are said to have been once Barons of Bealach (bràigh Dhail na Tràgha), but that during the Wars of Montrose they sold their lands and went to live in Lettermore at the foot of Beinn a' Bheithir. It is apparent that the name Solomon was in the family, for one of the Crown witnesses cited was Solomon MacColl, merchant in Auchindarroch. *Cf.* the Irish name MacSolly.

14 Donald Stewart, nephew and son-in-law of Ballachulish, aged about 30, was cited as a witness by the prosecution. He had been out in the '45 and had been wounded at Culloden.

15 John Stewart, 7th of Fasnacloich, described in the trial as " elder of Fasnacloich," was at this time 65 years old. This is probably James Stewart, 8th of Fasnacloich, aged 29 years, described as " younger of Fasnacloich." He had been wounded at Culloden.

16 11th May, 1752. The business in hand was to carry out evictions on the Mamore Estate.

17 There were actually with him his nephew, Mungo Campbell, writer in Edinburgh; Donald Kennedy, an Inverary Sheriff-officer; and Glenure's servant, John MacKenzie.

18 *i.e.*, the first ambush in Lochaber.

19 The ferryman at Ballachulish on the Appin side was Archibald MacInnes, aged 65 years. This is not the ferryman in question.

20 His actual words, according to Mungo Campbell's letter, were, " Oh! I'm dead; Mungo, take care of yourself; the villain's going to shoot you." The account given in Mungo Campbell's deposition is slightly different. The discrepancy may be due to the original having been in Gaelic.

21 " Glenure still kept his horse; and I removed him off, unable to utter a word, but opened his breast to show me the wound." (Mungo Campbell's letter, dated Fort William, 23rd May, 1752. (*Trial*, App. II, p. 304).

22 In the descriptions of Ailean Breac circulated at the time he is said to have " black bushy hair put up in a bag." (*Courant*, 28th May, 1752; *Trial*, App. IV, p. 308; *Courant*, 16th June, 1752; *Trial*, App. IV, p. 310).

23 This account is contrary to the recorded evidence. John Beg MacColl, servant to James Stewart, deponed that James went immediately to the door. (*Trial*, p. 172). Although it is not recorded that James was sowing barley on the 14th, Allan Stewart, his son, declared that he himself was sowing barley on the 12th of May (*v.* Allan Stewart's first declaration, *Trial*, p. 199). The oat sowing was pretty far advanced in the month of March (Dugald MacColl's deposition, *Trial*, p. 166). On the 14th of May the people of Auchindarroch were covering potatoes (Charles Stewart's fifth declaration, *Trial*, p. 206).

24 John Beg MacColl deponed that neither James Stewart nor any of his family went near the corpse; that James Stewart said that, as he and Glenure were not on good terms, and some of the people that were to meet Glenure had arms, he did not care to go near them, not knowing what might happen (*Trial*, p. 172). James Stewart himself declared that neither he nor his son, Allan, went there because he understood that Ballieveolan and his sons were to be there; " and there were some chagrine betwixt him and them, they having taken the declarant's possession the year before, wherein he had a stock of cattle, viz., Glenduror, a part of the estate of Ardsheil " (*Trial*, p. 195). Allan Stewart declared that his father wished to go and take care of the corpse, but that his (James') wife would not let him or the declarant go for fear of exciting the passions of Glenure's friends who might have arms (*Trial*, p. 201). Charles Stewart's declaration corroborated this (*Trial*, p. 206).

25 Alexander Campbell, in Teynaluib, deponed that " in the end of April last, the pannel called at the deponent's house in the morning, to have his horse corn'd; and having called for, and got a dram, which was afterwards set down upon the table, one Macclaren, a merchant in Stirling, who had lodged with the deponent the night before, being present, asked the pannel if he would not help the deponent to a dram. And the pannel answered, he did not know any thing that he would help the deponent, or any of his name to, if it was not to the gibbet. The deponent answered that was not a comfortable expression to him, that it seems if any of them were at the gibbet, the pannel would draw down their feet; and the pannel replied, that of some of them he would, and some of them he would not " (*Trial*, p. 159). The talk then turned to Glenure and the wrongs done to James. Colin MacLaren, merchant in Stirling, testified to the same effect, adding that James' answer was " that he did not chuse to be an executioner, but he could draw down some of them " (*Trial*, p. 161). In his speech from the gallows James Stewart asserted : " But this far I can safely say, upon the word of a Christian going into eternity, that I had no other intentions in what I said than a joke; and that if I had any grudge at himself for being Campbell I was under no necessity to go into his house, as there was another public-house within a gunshot of his door " (*Trial*, p. 296).

26 James Stewart and his son, Allan, were taken at first to Fort William, where they lay from the middle of May until the beginning of September, 1752. On October 5, after the trial, James was transferred to Fort William. On November 7 he was removed from Fort William to Ballachulish, where he was executed on the following day.

27 In a letter from Captain Alexander Campbell to his uncle (probably Sheriff Duncan Campbell), dated Glenure, 25th May, he says : " Phasanacloich has not been att home ever since this melancholy accident. I believe he is in Perthshire, and most probably amongst the Stewarts of Atholl. He was seen with Allan Breck, and stayed with him all Munday night att Balecheliss, and travelld with him on Teusday to Port Callart, none but he, I mean young Phasanacloich, in company ; there

61

are several other concurring circumstances too tedious to
mention here that makes it highly probable Phasanacloich
knew every step intended.''' In a postscript he adds: "I
think there ought (to be) a search made for Phasanacloich as
he is not at home, and we have a warrant against him."
(Trial, App. XIII, 1, p. 350).

28 The Court sat from September 21 until September 25, but the jury
actually framed its verdict on September 24.

29 This witness' evidence was regarded as the most damning against
James Stewart. John Breck MacColl, aged 40 years, married,
was bouman to Appin in Caolas nan Con (Deposition, Trial,
pp. 182-186). In addition to his deposition he made a
declaration (Trial, App. XVIII, 28, pp. 386-387). He is
referred to as John Don MacColl in a letter from Col. Crawfurd,
and as John Dow Breck MacColl in James Stewart's speech
from the scaffold. Captain Alexander Campbell, in a letter to
his father, dated Glenure, July 31st, 1752, writes: "Inver
says that Jon Breck was always Bred up about the Ardsheal
family till Whitsunday, 1751, when at James particular desire
Appin without consulting him made him his Bowman" (Trial,
App. XVIII, 25, p. 384). Andrew Lang says that, until
recently, the MacColls were disliked for the part played by
this witness and were named "King George's MacColls"
(Historical Mysteries, p. 78).

30 There are indications that bribes and threats were used on both
sides in this case. It appears from the correspondence relating
to the case that John Breck MacColl, the bouman, had been
interviewed by James Stewart's friends and threatened, and
that he asked the authorities to arrest him so as to make him
appear an unwilling witness and thus save him from the
Stewarts' ire (v. letter from Col. Crawfurd, Trial, App. XVIII,
14, p. 377). Hugh Maclean, barber in Maryburgh, deponed
that James Stewart had said that he "was afraid of
nothing but that his servants might be inticed to take money,
and turn against him; and desired the deponent, as from him,
to tell his servants to say nothing but truth, to keep their
minds to themselves, and he would take care of them" (Trial,
p. 187). This remark, arising from a very understandable
solicitude on James' part, was gravely misconstrued by the
prosecution. That these servants, to be used as witnesses in
the trial, lay in prison at Fort William, was highly irregular.
In his speech from the scaffold James said that "all the poor
people were put in such a terror by a military force kept in

62

different parts of the country that they—I mean the poor
country people—would say whatever they thought pleased my
prosecutors best " (Trial, p. 293). He said that John Beg
MacColl was persuaded on the way to Inverary, with the help
of some aqua vitæ, to make up a story which would seriously
damage him, James Stewart. He added that he was assured
that plenty of bribes or rewards had been offered to several;
that Donald Ranken, herd to Ballachulish, had been offered
eighteen hundred merks and that he was kept a close prisoner
at Inverary, so that none of his (James') friends had access to
put any questions to him; that John MacCombich, late miller
in the mill of Ardsheil, was offered his former possession of
the mill for telling anything would answer their turn; and
that Duncan MacCombich and Duncan MacColl, both in
Lagnaha, were offered as much meal as they pleased to call
for at Fort William if they would make any discoveries.
(Trial, p. 294). The enormous costs of the trial, amounting
to £1334 9s 2½d, to which objections were made, seem to
corroborate all this. The author of the Supplement declared
that " not only James Stewart's friends were menaced, but the
whole country put under terror " (Trial, App. VIII, p. 332).
He also mentioned that some of the witnesses had lain in
shackles at Fort William.

31 Duncan Campbell, change-keeper at Annat, deponed that Allan
Breck had said that " if the deponent had any respect for his
friends, he would tell them, that if they offered to turn out
the possessors of Ardsheil's estate, he would make black cocks
of them before they entered into possession, by which the
deponent understood shooting them, it being a common phrase
in the country " (Trial, p. 139). John Breck MacColl deponed
that " in a conversation the deponent had with the pannel
(i.e., James Stewart), as the deponent best remembers, about
two years ago, mention being made of Glenure's being about
to take on the management of the estate of Ardsheil from the
said pannel, and thereby disabling the pannel from being of
any service to Ardsheil's children, he heard the pannel say,
he would be willing to spend a shot upon Glenure, tho' he
went upon his knees to his window to fire it " (Trial, p. 186;
v. also an unsigned letter, App. XVIII, 18, p. 379). John
Breck MacColl did not mention this threat in his declaration
(v. Trial, App. XVIII, 28, pp. 386-7); and James Stewart denied
it in his speech from the scaffold, pointing out that, at the
time he was supposed to have uttered it, he was on friendly
terms with Glenure (Trial, p. 293).

32 Mr Mackay, in his notes on the local traditions respecting the murder, says that one person had to be bound with ropes by his family to prevent his going to the scaffold on the fatal morning to make the facts known (*Trial*, App. XVII, p. 367).

33 He denied it on several occasions (*v*. Introd. to this Tale).

34 Archibald, 3rd Duke of Argyll, died on 15th April, 1761. He was succeeded as 4th Duke, and in his Scottish Estates, by his cousin, John Campbell of Mamore (1761-1770). The Duke referred to here, however (in order to square with the Laird of Ballachulish mentioned), must be John, 5th Duke of Argyll (1770-1806), who was " Commander in Chief of His Majestys fforces in Scotland and garisons in North Britain." (*Highland Papers*, Vol. II, p. 111).

35 In 1755 the skeleton fell from the gibbet, but it was replaced again after an investigation had established that its fall had been due to the wind.

36 This must refer to John Stewart, 5th of Ballachulish, described in the trial as " younger of Ballachulish." He succeeded his father, Alexander Stewart, 4th of Ballachulish, who died in 1774. John Stewart died in 1794.

37 Colin Campbell of Glenure had a brother, Alexander, who was an officer in the army, but he was not Laird of Barcaldine. He had also a nephew, Alexander Campbell, son of his eldest brother, John Campbell of Barcaldine (*ob*. 1777). Alexander died in 1779, but never succeeded to his father's estates, as they had been bought from his father by his uncle, Duncan Campbell, who died in 1784. In the *Index to the Tales* the person who took part in the Rannoch hunt is described as " Alasdair mac Bharra-challtuinn " (Alexander, son of Barcaldine).

38 Mr Mackay, in his notes on the local traditions regarding the murder, tells that, years after the murder, a young girl, Janet MacInnes, found a gun in the hollow of a large elder tree. She showed it to old Mr Stewart of Ballachulish, who remarked, " 'S e sin gunna dubh a' mhi-fhortain, a Sheònaid " (that is the black gun of the misfortune, Janet). He says that the gun was known in the district as "An t-Slinneanach," and that it is still, or was recently, kept as an interesting and awesome relic in a private house in the Ballachulish district. (*Trial*, App. XVII, p. 369).